Must Know Literary Works of 20th Century: A Competitive Exam Companion to Ace NET/SET in English Literature

Dr. SHERLIN SMILE

CONTENTS

Dedicated to Family and Students.

Contents

39. Things Fall Apart

40. Disgrace

41. The English Patient

42. The Handmaid's Tale

43. Surfacing

44. One Hundred Years of Solitude

45. Lolita

46. The Trial

47. The Metamorphosis

48. The Tin Drum

49. The Good Earth

50. The Guide

51. Swami and Friends

52. Kanthapura

53. Nectar in a Sieve

54. Train to Pakistan

55. The Namesake

56. The Inheritance of Loss

57. The Shadow Lines

58. The Hungry Tide

59. The White Tiger

CONTENTS

Foreword

This book stands as a testament to the enduring legacy of English literature, providing readers with a collection of scholarly synopses of seminal works of twentieth century that have shaped the literary landscape. Each synopsis offers a concise yet informed overview of these masterpieces, serving not only as an introduction to the works themselves but also as a gateway to the rich thematic and stylistic diversity that defines the English literary tradition.

In exploring these works—from the haunting depths of Joseph Conrad's Heart of Darkness to the complex postcolonial imagination of Salman Rushdie's Midnight's Children—the reader is invited to journey through time, across continents, and into the minds of some of the greatest literary figures. The synopses in this book do more than summarize; they encapsulate the essence of each work, highlighting central themes, significant characters, and the broader cultural and historical contexts that have influenced and been influenced by these texts.

The selection covers a broad spectrum of genres and styles, reflecting the evolution of literary forms and the shifting concerns of society over the centuries. Whether it is the exploration of moral ambiguity, the critique of imperialism, or the profound examination of the human psyche, these works continue to resonate with readers, offering timeless insights into the human condition.

As you engage in a discourse with the pages that follow, may you find inspiration, experience enlightenment, and perhaps discover or rediscover the profound impact these literary treasures have had on our world. This book is a celebration of the power of words and the enduring influence of the English literary canon.

This book is a must-have in the backpack of any young intellectual explorer who wishes to traverse the vast literary landscape of English literature, all in the hope of finding that magical land of a lucrative career.

Dr A. S. Mohanagiri

Associate Professor in English

Government Arts College Coimbatore.

Preface

It is a small book designed exclusively for NET/ SET aspirants and students preparing for competitive exams. The book is designed to help the students to navigate on the important and must know facts about the of the greatest works of literature in twentieth century Its chief purpose is to provide the aspirants a short overview on the works of literature.

This book imparts a short summary and guidance on key authors and their works which are commonly tested in competitive exams. The goal of this book is to equip the aspirants and students with the necessary details about great authors and works to excel in competitive exams.

This book provides

- Information about the genre of the work of art
- Offers detailed explanation on characters and their significance
- Familiarize with the setting of the work and theme
- Highlights the important quotes and famous adaptations

This book is a companion to ace NET/SET and competitive exams. I wish all the best for the aspirants and wishing you all success in your exams.

Dr.SHERLIN SMILE

Acknowledgments

I thank the Almighty God for showering His blessings in my endeavour to make this work a fruitful one.

I here with record my profound gratitude to **Dr.A.S. Mohanagiri** for inspiring me to write and for instilling confidence in me. I express a sincere and whole hearted thanks to my friend **Dr. Ganesh Muthuram,** CIT, Coimbatore for his unwavering support and encouragement throughout this process.

I express my wholehearted thanks to my husband **A.Jerold** for the continuous support and encouragement that have been a constant source of strength and inspiration .

Dr. Sherlin Smile

1. Heart of Darkness(1902)

AUTHOR: Joseph Conrad, Polish descent and his original name is Jozef Korzeniowski.

GENRE: It is a Novella, which belongs to the genre of colonial literature; **fame story**, a story inside story with an anonymous narrator.

PUBLICATION: Published in 1899 serially in three issues of Blackwood's *Edinburgh Magazine* and also published in 1902 as a third work in the anthology "*Youth.*"

PLOT: The plot centers around the main character and protagonist Charles Marlow, a sailor who was journeying up in the Congo River in a boat called Nelly to meet a mysterious white man Kurtz, who by his eloquence and hypnotic personality dominates the tribal people and has employed divergent means and methods of consistently getting ivory from the interior parts of Africa and to relieve him.

MAJOR CHARACTERS: Marlow, the protagonist, steamer pilot, who is excited and interested in exploring the "unexplored"; **Kurtz**, the object of Marlow's quest; **The Jungle,** the antagonist; **Russian,** a Young man whom Marlow calls 'gallantly thoughtlessly alive'; **Helmsman**, a proud athlete who Marlow mentions as an 'unstable fool.'

THEMES: Greed and Imperialism; Hypocrisy and Indifference, Racism, Savagery vs Civilization.

SETTING: The novella was set in the 19th century Belgian controlled Congo Free state, the deck of the *nellie,* the Congo River.

SIGNIFICANCE OF TITLE: The title alludes not only to the mysteries of Africa, "the dark continent" but also to the heart of evil, ignorance and fear residing in the human heart.

SYMBOLS: *Darkness*, *Ivory* symbolise the greed of Europeans, *Harlequim*, *Congo River*, symbolize Marlow's journey to self.

ADAPTATIONS: The book was the inspiration for Francis Ford Coppola's Vietnam War film *Apocalypse Now* (1979).

REVIEWS/CRITICISM: Chinua Achebe, deemed the book as racist for its portrayal of native African cultures.

QUOTES

"We live, as we dream—alone."

"Exterminate all the brutes!"

"There is a taint of death, a flavor of mortality in lies."

"The horror! The horror!"

POINTS TO REMEMBER

- Conrad presents two conflicting discourses of the same culture Anti colonialism and Eurocentrism in the novella (Sep 2013 Net).

- The novel begins with River Thames(Aug 2016).

- Marlow concludes the novella by telling a lie to Kurtz's Fiancé that the last word Kurtz uttered was her name

- Kurtz dies by crying "horror! Horror!"

- This novella reflects the physical and psychological shock Conrad experienced, when he was working in the Belgian Congo in 1890.

- Joseph Conrad condemns the Western imperialism—of the greed, violence, and exploitation in the name of adventures to bring "light" and civilization to the "dark" and needy areas of the world.

- The novel has been widely appreciated for its poignant look at the destructive influence of colonization on the colonized and colonizer.

2. Lord Jim (1900)

AUTHOR: Joseph Conrad, Polish-British Novelist

GENRE: Psychological novel

PUBLICATION: Originally published as a serial in *Blackwood's Magazine* from October 1899 to November 1900

SIGNIFICANCE OF TITLE: The title refers to the novel's central character, a disgraced seaman whose quest for redemption earns him the title "Lord Jim".

PLOT: The story revolves around Jim, a promising young man who ventures to sea with the dream of becoming a hero, becomes a coward, desserts the passengers in danger in the vessel Patna overcomes the haunts of Patna by sacrificing his life for natives as a spiritual leader.

MAJOR CHARACTERS: Jim, the hero, who strictly adheres to the moral code of behavior; **Captain Marlow**, an experienced trainer who trains Jim; **Breirly** famously known as "Big Brierly" Stein; **Brown**, son of a low ranking English Baronet calls him "Gentleman Brown"; **Jewel**, Jim's beloved.

THEMES: Lost Honor, Exile, Illusions versus Reality, Trust vs Betrayal.

SETTING: The novel is set in Malign, Patna, port in the Red Sea.

SYMBOLS: Jim's Jump refers to the descent and fall from grace, **Butterflies,** it represents an embodiment of idealism, **Brierly's Gold Chronometer** represents civilized virtues, **The Ship Patna** symbolises the path of a soul.

REVIEWS/CRITICISM

- Conrad's modernist style and use of antiheroes proved a significant influence on other 20th-century American writers, including William Faulkner, F. Scott Fitzgerald, and Ernest Hemingway, and English novelist Graham Greene.

- In 1925, Fitzgerald stated he had used Conrad's literary style in writing his masterpiece *The Great Gatsby* (1925), modeling narrator Nick Carraway on Conrad's Marlow.

QUOTES

"Man is born a coward."

"He was imprisoned within the very freedom of his power."

POINTS TO REMEMBER

- Jim was shot to death by Dorimean in the end of the novel (June2013 NET)

- The novel ends as "He feels it himself and stays often he is preparing to leave all these and preparing to leave while he waves his hands sadly at the butterflies(Dec 2013)

- Conrad sets his three works, *Almayer's Folly, Outcast of the Sea and Lord Jim* in Malign.

- Conrad examines the cost of human weakness and moral failings in Lord Jim

- Conrad applies innovative techniques such as nonlinear time-shifts and multiple perspectives that reflect multiple truth and stands as groundbreaking bridge between the Victorian and modernist periods.

- The opening event in the novel *Lord Jim* is based in part on an actual abandonment of a ship on 17 July 1880, S.S. *Jeddah* sailed from Singapore bound for Penang and Jeddah, with 778 men, 147 women and 67 children on board.

- The bulk of the novel is told in the form of a story recited by the character Marlow to a group of listeners, and the conclusion is presented in the form of a letter from Marlow. Within Marlow's narration, other characters also tell their own stories in nested dialogue. Thus, events in the novel are described from several viewpoints, and often out of chronological order.

- The novel begins in a third-person, omniscient voice, with a close view of Jim's inner life, and then shifts to a clear narrator, Marlow.

- **"He is one of us"**, the statement asserted by Marlow establishes solidarity and captures different connotation with each usage.

- **Man is not a masterpiece",** a statement made by Stein as he studies his butterflies in Marlow's presence

3. Look Back in Anger

AUTHOR: John Osborne

GENRE: Realistic play, Angry Young man theatre

TITLE: The plot revolves around the complex emotional state of the central character, Jimmy Porter, who expresses the outrageous political and social condition of post World War II England.

PLOT: Jimmy porter, the protagonist who is angry at his country, his wife, his dead-end job, his seemingly hopeless future is an intelligent and educated but disaffected young man of working-class origin. It portrays his marital struggle with his wife, Alison Porter, who belongs to the upper class.

MAJOR CHARACTERS: Jimmy Porter, an educated young man of post World War II; **Alison Porter** is a young educated woman of upper class society and wife of Jimmy; **Cliff Lewis** ,an old friend of Jimmy shares a similar background of Jimmy; **Helena Charles**, an old friend of Alison.

SETTING: The play is set in the One-Room Flat of Jimmy in English Highlands.

ADAPTATIONS: The play was adapted into a motion picture by Tony Richardson in 1959 under the same title starring Richard Burton and Mary Ure. Film production credited Circa 1958.

SYMBOLS: ***Teddy Bear and Squirrel***, is a metaphor of Jimmy and Alison relationship, ***Newspaper*** represents emptiness in the contemporary society, ***Trumpet***, is a symbol of freedom

THEMES: Real life and Real Pain, upper class and middle Class

QUOTES

"Common as dirt that's me" - jimmy

"Let's pretend that we're human beings and that we're alive" - Jimmy

"If only...something would happen…. to wake you out of your beauty sleep"

POINTS TO REMEMBER

- John Osborne started the phenomena of angry Youngman with the characterisation of Jimmy Porter
- Jimmy provokes his wife Alison by calling her Pusillanimous (timid and cowardly)
- Through Jimmy Osborne expresses the two primary emotions, rebelliousness and restlessness of the period (Sep 2013)NET
- Sequel to Look Back in Anger is Déjàvu - Jimmy in Middle Ages
- This play is the First in the category of Kitchen Sink Drama

4. The Playboy of the Western World (1907)

AUTHOR: John Millington Synge, an Irish Playwright

Related to Irish Literary Renaissance

GENRE: Drama

TITLE:J. M. Synge's *The Playboy of the Western World*, the "Western" part of the title refers to the West of Ireland.

 PLOT: It is a story of Christy Mahon, a brag who claimed that he has killed his father. Christy's tale succeeds in capturing the romantic attention of the bar-maid Pegeen Mike, the daughter of Flaherty and the villagers.

THEMES: Dream and Reality, Patricide and Self Discovery of Christy, Darkness, Heroism, Power of Language, Authority,

MAJOR CHARACTERS: Christopher "Christy" Mahon -is the central character of the play; **Pegeen Mike**, whose full name is Margaret Flaherty, a bar-maid; **Widow Quin** – a woman in thirties; **Old Mahon**,Christy's Father; **Michael James Flaherty**, Pegeen's Father.

SETTING: Michael James Flaherty's public house in County Mayo (on the west coast of Ireland) A pub in the Northwestern Ireland, circa

ADAPTATIONS

- *The Playboy of the Western World* was adapted for television in 1946 by the BBC and in 1983 in Ireland.

- A film version of *The Playboy of the Western World* was produced and directed by Brian Hurstin Ireland in 1962, starring Siobhan McKenna and Gary Raymond.

SYMBOLS: The Loy, it is a type of narrow spade used in Ireland for cultivating potatoes, represents the repetitive labour of Irish folk, ***Christy*** symbolizes Christ who is praised and then betrayed.

QUOTES

"A "daring fellow is the jewel of the world...." —Michael Flaherty

"Oh my grief, I've lost him surely. I've lost the only Playboy of the Western World." —Pegeen Mike

POINTS TO REMEMBER

- *The Playboy of the Western World*, was highly controversial as it tries to portray rural Irish life and language, causing riots in its first performances in 1907 due to the perception that it was unfairly degrading to the Irish people, especially Irish womanhood
- *Brian Friel's 1980 play Translations* makes for an interesting counterpoint to *The Playboy of the Western World*; which centers on issues of language, Irish history, and English colonialism

- The play stems from a story or stories Synge heard while on the Aran Isles, west of the coast of Ireland. For example, the moment in which Pegeen Mike accuses Widow Quin of having reared a black ram at her "own breast" was based on a story told to Synge by a landlord in West Kerry
- The play is known for lyrical speeches in Irish
- The phrase 'Playboy of The Western World' is used by Widow Quin in a sarcastic way to taunt Christy after the revelation by Christy's father

5. Riders to the Sea (1904)

AUTHOR: John Millington Synge

GENRE: One- Act Tragedy

TITLE: The title *"Riders to the Sea"* symbolically highlights the main themes of the play, conflict between man and the sea. It provokes the readers to know who the riders to the sea are.

THEMES: Spirituality and Mourning, Fate and Mortality, Age and Gender, the Power of the Sea

PLOT: Synge's one-act play is a compressed tragedy of an elderly mother Maurya, a poor peasant and fisher folk of the Aran Island, who has lost her husband, and five of her sons to the sea. The plot revolves around the hopeless struggle of people like Maurya against the impersonal but relentless cruelty of the sea.

MAJOR CHARACTERS: Maurya, an old woman, is the mother of **Bartley; Michael, Cathleen and Nora Bartley** is Maurya's last surviving son; **Cathleen**, is Maurya's older daughter; **The Young Priest**, who never appears physically in the play but being referred by other characters; **Michael,** is Maurya's son who disappeared before the play; **The Sea**, the antagonist

SETTING: Aran Islands, Inishmaan

ADAPTATIONS: It was adapted into a 40-minute black-and-white Irish Film in 1935 directed by Brian Desmond Hurst with screenplay adaptation by Patrick Kirwan with Sara Allgood

SYMBOLS: The main symbol is **Sea** which symbolises both the source and destroyer of life, **The Riders** represents the man's defeat before natural power, ***Bartley's Horses*** symbolise death and fate, ***The White Boards***, is an omen of death, ***The Rope***, is also a symbol of death

QUOTES

"I hung it up this morning, for the pig with the black feet was eating it"

"What more can we want than that? No man at all can be living for ever, and we must be satisfied."

POINTS TO REMEMBER

- W.B. Yeats encouraged Synge to travel to the Aran Islands and he stayed there from 1898 - 1902 collecting materials and observed the people who lived there
- Synge wrote this play Riders to the Sea inspired by the story of a man from Inishmaan whose body washed up on the shore of an island of County Donegal
- All his plays were produced in Abbey theatre, in which he became a director in 1906
- His last work Deirdre of sorrow was finished by Yeats and his fiancee Molly Allgood

6. The Forsyte Saga (1906- 1921)

AUTHOR: John Galsworthy

GENRE: Fiction, Sentimental Domestic Comedy, Social Novel.

TITLE: *The Forsyte Saga* is a sequence of five texts which includes three original novels -- *The Man of Property(1918), In Chancery(1920), and To Let(1921)* -- and their connecting interludes, *Indian Summer of a Forsyte and Awakening.*

THEMES : Materialism, Extreme Individualism, Egoism, A Strong Sense of Property, Money Worship.

PLOT: The saga chronicles trace the decline of fortune of three generations of a moneyed middle-class English Forsyte family at the turn of the century.**Soames Forsyte,** the nephew of 'old Jolyon' a solicitor and *"man of property,"* is married to the beautiful, penniless Irene, who rebels against his values. She falls in love with Philip Bosinney, the French architect whom Soames had hired to build a country house. Soames rapes Irene, whom he considers his property, and proceeds to ruin Bosinney, who subsequently dies in a traffic accident in London. Irene returns to Soames.

*In Chancery*concerns the love between Irene and Young Jolyon Forsyte, Soames's cousin. (The story of the last days of Old Jolyon, his father, is told in "Indian Summer of a Forsyte.") Irene and Soames divorce; she marries Jolyon and bears a son, Jon. Concurrently, Soames marries Annette Lamotte, have a daughter, Fleur.

In *To Let*, Fleur and Jon grow up and fall in love; Jolyon informs his son of Irene and Soames's past relationship. Although Fleur is determined to marry Jon, he refuses. Fleur becomes the wife of Michael Mont, son of a baronet. Young Jolyon dies, and Irene leaves England to join Jon in America. Soames discovers that Annette is involved in an affair with a Frenchman, Belgian, as Irene and found that Irene's house ,Robin Hill is empty and to let.

MAJOR CHARACTERS:

First Generation Forsytes

- **Ann**, the eldest of the family
- **Old Jolyon**, the eldest brother, made a fortune in tea

Second Generation Forsytes

- **Young Jolyon,** Old Jolyon's artistic and free-thinking son, married three times.
- **Soames**, James and Emily's son, an intense, unimaginative and possessive solicitor, married to the unhappy Irene, who later marries Young Jolyon

Third Generation

- **Yon,** Young Jolyon's son from his third marriage, to Irene, Soames's first wife

- **Fleur,** Soames's daughter from his second marriage, to a French Sohoshopgirl Annette; Jon's lover; later marries the heir of a baronet, Michael Mont

ADAPTATIONS

It was serialised in BBC in 26 episodes in 1967 and was adapted Granada Television for the ITV network   in 2002

QUOTES

"One's eyes are what one is, one's mouth is what one becomes."

"He might wish and wish and never get it - the beauty and the loving in the world!"

"Love is not a hot-house flower, but a wild plant, born of a wet night, born of an hour of sunshine; sprung from wild seed, blown along the road by a wild wind. A wild plant that, when it blooms by chance within the hedge of our gardens, we call a flower; and when it blooms outside we call a weed; but, flower or weed, whose scent and colour are always, wild!"

POINTS TO REMEMBER

- Galsworthy's own sequel to *The Forsyte Saga* came as *A Modern Comedy*, written in the years 1924 to 1928.This comprises a novel, *The White Monkey*, an interlude, *A*

Silent Wooing, a second novel, *The Silver Spoon*, a second interlude, *Passers By*, and a third novel, *Swan Song*

- *The Forsyte Saga* earned John Galsworthy the Nobel Prize for Literature in 1932.
- Until 1904 he published his works under the pseudonym John Sinjohn
- He addressed class system and social issues like George Bernard Shaw in his plays *The Strife and The Skin Game*
- The character Irene is drawn from Ada Pearson his wife

7. *Kipps: The Story of a Simple Soul* (1905)

AUTHOR: H.G. Wells(Herbert George Wells)

GENRE: Social novel, a Bildungsroman novel, it is a literary genre that focuses on the psychological and moral growth of the protagonist from youth to the maturity of adulthood.

THEMES: Fear, Supernatural, Revenge, Isolation and the Conspiracy of Silence.

PLOT: Artie Kipps orphaned at an early age, raised by his aunt and uncle, and apprenticed for seven years to a draper, Artie Kipps is stunned to discover upon reading a newspaper advertisement that he is the grandson of a wealthy gentleman - and the inheritor of his fortune. Thrown dramatically into the upper classes, he struggles desperately to learn the etiquette and rules of polite society. But as he soon discovers, becoming a 'true gentleman' is neither as easy nor as desirable as it at first appears. Humorous yet sympathetic, the perceptive <u>social novel</u> is generally regarded as a masterpiece.

MAJOR CHARACTERS: Arthur Kipps, the protagonist whose birth is mysterious; **Ann Pornick,** Kipps love and wife,

ADAPTATIONS: It was adapted into the stage and cinema musical *Half a Sixpence.*

- *In 1984, Michelene Wandor dramatised it for BBC Radio 4, starring Paul Daneman and Mark Straker.*

REVIEWS/CRITICISM: Arnold Bennett, the famous English novelist commended that the book showed "ferocious hostility to about five-sixths of the characters"

8. Nineteen Eighty-Four (1949)

AUTHOR: George Orwell , his original name is Eric Arthur Blair (George(patron saint) Orwell (Favorite River)

GENRE: Science Fiction, Dystopian Fiction, Social Science Fiction, Fantasy Fiction, Political Fiction.

TITLE: Orwell confers this title to symbolise the future on the request of the publisher as 1984. He actually planned to call his novel "The Last Man in Europe".

THEMES: Totalitarianism ,Class Struggle ,Freedom vs Oppression ,Fear and Hate As Means Of Control, Individual Thought vs Mind Control.

PLOT: Winston Smith, the protagonist of the novel, is a rank-and-file Party member, an outwardly diligent and skillful worker who longs for truth and decency. Gradually he started hating the party and dreams of being a rebellion against Big Brother. To portray his rebel to the party he entered into a forbidden relationship with his co - worker Julia.

MAJOR CHARACTERS: Winston Smith , the hero without heroic qualities, a 39-year-old member of the Outer Party, who works at the Ministry of Truth; **Big Brother**, the mustachioed figurehead and supreme leader of the Party; **O'Brien**, a prominent member of the Inner Party; **Julia**, introduced as "the dark-haired girl" who works in the Fiction Department of the Ministry of Truth; **Emmanuel Goldstein** ,an early leader of Big Brother's; **Mr. Charrington** ,a frail sextuagenarian, who owns an antique shop.

SETTING: Orwell sets this novel in Oceania, an imagined future in 1984.

SYMBOLS: *Emmanuel Goldstein* symbolises power of group thinking, *The Telescreen*, symbolizes the continuous surveillance of the people by the party, *Newspeak and the Memory Hole* symbolize   the   party's   total   thought   control.   ***Big Brother*** symbolises the party itself, **2 + 2 = 5** is a symbol of lie in the party.

QUOTES

      "It was a bright cold day in April, and the clocks were striking thirteen"(Nov-2013 NET)

      "Big Brother Is Watching You."

      "War is peace. Freedom is slavery. Ignorance is strength."

      "Freedom is the freedom to say that two plus two make four."

      "Power is not a means; it is an end"

POINTS TO REMEMBER

- Many of its terms and concepts, such as Big Brother, doublethink, thoughtcrime, Newspeak, Room 101, telescreen, 2 + 2 = 5, and memory hole, have entered into common usage since its publication in 1949

- *Nineteen Eighty-Four* also popularised the adjective Orwellian

- George Orwell says "Where I lack the political purpose I wrote lifeless books"(June 2013 (Net)

- Young Eris lives in Trading town in katha (Dec 2013)

9. *Animal Farm (1945)*

AUTHOR: George Orwell

GENRE: Allegorical Novella, Political Satire

TITLE: *Animal Farm,* and Snowball teaches them the principles of Animalism, which promote equality and integrity. The renaming of the farm is significant because it illustrates the animals' control over their dominion and future.

THEMES: Leadership and Corruption, Power of Language, Corruption of Ideals, Totalitarianism, Lies and Deception, Dreams and Hopes, Leadership and Corruption.

PLOT: *Animal Farm* is a satire in beast fable, where the animals of Mr. Jones' stable revolt against their human masters and drive them out .The plot revolves around Napoleon , the pig, the chief and egalitarian leader who was corrupted by power and becomes tyrannical.

MAJOR CHARACTERS: Napoleon, the pig who emerge as a leader after the rebellion; **Snowball**, the pig who challenges Napoleon; **Boxer**, a cat-horse of incredible strength; **Squealer**, the pig who propaganda; **Old Major,** prize winning Boar.

SETTING: The Manor Farm in England

SYMBOLS: Manor Farm, the name of the animal farm symbolises the revolutionary Russia, **The Barn** represents the collective memory of a modern nation, **The Windmill** represents the administration of the pigs, **Whiskey** represents corruption, **The Seven Commandments of Animalism** represent the power of propaganda, **Milk and Apples** are symbols for richness.

QUOTES: "Four legs good, two legs bad."

"All animals are equal, but some are more equal than others."

POINTS TO REMEMBER

- The ultimate commandment in the novel is **All animals are equal, but some are more equal than others.**

10.Ulysses (1922)

AUTHOR: James Joyce - Irish novelist

GENRE: Fiction

TITLE: *Ulysses* is named after Odysseus ("Ulysses" is the Latin version of his name), the hero of the Greek epic poem *The Odyssey*, attributed to the poet Homer.

THEMES: Sex, Love, and Everyday Empathy, Fathers and Sons, Irish Nationalism and the Catholic Church, Femininity and Maternity, Death, Exoticism

PLOT: *Ulysses* records events in the lives of two central characters--Leopold Bloom and Stephen Dedalus--on June 16 1904,a day and a night(the anniversary of Joyce first walk with his wife Nora Barnacle) a single day in Dublin. With its depth and complexities, Ulysses completely changed our understanding of literature and language.

MAJOR CHARACTERS: Bloom, a Jewish advertising canvasser, who is a seller of newspaper ads and an impresario; **Molly,** wife of Bloom and daughter of an Irish officer; **Major Tweedy, Stephen Dedalus,** an intelligent and self-absorbed college graduate.

SETTING: Set in 1904, Irish Free State Dublin, Ireland.

SYMBOLS: Crossed Keys stands for fatherhood and Security, **Throwaway** stands for Bloom's triumph over Boylan, **Bloom's Potato** represents protection from danger.

QUOTES

"It lay beneath him, a bowl of bitter"

"What does Shakespeare say? Put but money in thy purse."

"Elijah is coming! ... Is coming! Is coming!! Is coming!!!"

"Coming events cast their shadows before."

"You will not be the master of others nor the slave."

POINTS TO REMEMBER

- June 16 is celebrated today as 'Bloomsday'
- Leopald Bloom represents Odysseus ,Stephen represents ulysses, Molly represents Penelope
- The 18 chapters coincide with the episodes of Odysseus
- The last chapter is an extended monologue by Molly
- Virginia woolf comments that "Ulysses is a Misfire" - (NET)
- Joyce uses the form of expressionist drama(ie, play - script like passages meant to be read and emphasizes emotional experience rather than events in the external world, and puppets and other props)to reveal truths about Bloom's and Stephen's inner worlds, echoing Freud's theories on sexuality, repression, and the subconscious mind
- In the "Penelope" episode Joyce uses interior monologue to represent Molly's thoughts directly. Her Interior monologue

moves through the story of her whole life—girlhood, her marriage to Bloom, her affair with Boylan, and everything in between

- Parallax life, Joyce makes use of the device in juxtapositions of characters, their different perspectives of the same event. Parallax in science and literature speak to the same phenomenon: an object or event viewed from different perspectives will result in different views
- *Ulysses* is sometimes seen as the modernist masterpiece of a literary technique called stream of consciousness.
- Ulysses was initially published without chapter numbers or chapter titles. The 18 chapters (called "episodes")
- Joyce's "Cyclops" episode makes numerous parallels with Homer's Odyssey. The episode is full of images of eyes and blindness
- Episode I - Telemacus and episode 18 - Penelope
- The final word in Ulysses is "YES" (NET)

11. A Portrait of the Artist as a Young Man (1916)

AUTHOR: James Joyce , an Irish modernist Writer

GENRE:Kunstleroman(growth of an artist in the novel).
Autobiographical

TITLE: The title, *A Portrait of the Artist as a Young Man*, signals
the main character, Stephen Dedalus, who develops as an artist in
this self portrait.

THEMES: Inspiration, Inner Conflict, Spiritual Homelessness

PLOT: A Portrait of an artist as a young man describes Stephen
Dedalus's development from a bright young student to a gradual
sense of his destiny as a dedicated artist.

MAJOR CHARACTERS: Stephen Dedalus, the protagonist a
sensitive young and a budding artist; **Simon Dedalus,** a week
sentimental father of Stephen; **Mary Dedalus**, Stephen's mother
who is very pious; **Cranly**, a friend of Stephen.

SETTING: Ireland

ADAPTATIONS: Ezra Pound published this book serially in his magazine "Egoist"

A film version adapted for the screen by Judith Rascoe and directed by Joseph Strick was released in 1977.

SYMBOLS: Colors represent opposite views of stephen, **Stephen Dedalus** represents the high aspiration of the hero, **Wading Girl** symbolizes   artistic ideal, **Writing** symbolises Stephen's awareness to unique vision

QUOTES

"In the soft grey silence he could hear the bump of the balls: and ...the cricket bats: pick, pack, pock, puck: like drops of water in a fountain falling softly in the brimming bowl."

"The ambition which he felt astir at sought no outlet."

"A cold lucid indifference reigned in his soul."

POINTS TO REMEMBER:

- *A Portrait of the Artist as a Young Man* is told from a limited omniscient point of view; the narrator's thoughts mirror those of the main character, Stephen Dedalus

- Stephen Dedalus has epiphanic moments of realisation one such is that he has no zeal for priesthood

- "Once upon a time and a very good time it was there was a moocow coming down along the road and this moocow that was coming down along the road met a nicens little boy named baby tuckoo …" -Opening line of *A Portrait of the Artist as a Young Man*

- *T*he first title given to it by Joyce is "Stephen Hero"
- Harriet Shaw Weaver is the lifelong benefactress of Joyce

12. To the Lighthouse (1927)

AUTHOR: Virginia Woolf

GENRE: Drama

TITLE: *To the Lighthouse,* the title signifies the journey of the Mrs.Ramsay's family to the lighthouse which signifies the quest for values. And it is also about the characters strive to achieve the unattainable.

THEMES: Love and Loss, Internal Life, Reality versus the Ideal

PLOT: The plot is divided into three parts (ie, Window, Time passes and Lighthouse)which Virginia woolf defines as "H" shaped. The serene and maternal Mrs. Ramsay, the tragic yet absurd Mr. Ramsay, and their eight children with their assorted guests are on holiday on the Isle of Skye. The plot centers around the desire of the youngest to visit the nearby lighthouse and the father's seemingly trivial postponement to it.   The book is an amalgam of grief, rapture, tragedy, comedy, tyranny, conflict and all the complexities of family life.

MAJOR CHARACTERS: Mrs. Ramsay, Mother of eight, an advocate for marriage and family; **Mr. Ramsay,** a profound philosopher; **Lily Briscoe**, a free - spirited painter; **James,** the younger one, who wants to go the lighthouse from the beginning;

Cam, the rebellious son; **Paul Rayley,** the young friend of Ramsay; **Minta Doyle** , a guest who evokes Mrs Ramsay's jealousy.

SETTING: Isle of Skye in Scotland between 1910 and 1920.

ADAPTATIONS: In 1983, *To the Lighthouse* was made into a telefilm starring Rosemary Harris, Michael Gough, Suzanne Bertish, and Kenneth Branagh.

SYMBOLS: Lighthouse represents the inaccessibility of the family, permanence, order, **The Painting** represents understanding and catharsis, **The Tree** represents love, life and protection

QUOTES

> "It was a thousand pities."
> "Love had a thousand shapes."
> "Everything seemed possible. Everything seemed right."

POINTS TO REMEMBER

- It drawn on her memory of family holidays at St.Ives, Cornwall
- The novel has three sections" The Window", " Time Passes", " To the lighthouse"

- This novel is the key example of the literary technique called multiple focalization, where the novel has few dialogue and almost no action and most of the actions are presented as thoughts and observations.
- Lily Brisco, a painter who is in the act of painting is portrayed as a character by Woolf (June 2012)(June 2015)
- The novel concludes as "It was done , it was finished yes she thought lying down the brush in extreme fatigue I have had my vision (Dec2013)

13.Orlando: A Biography (1928)

AUTHOR: Virginia Woolf

GENRE: Satire

TITLE: It is an allusion to the Shakespearean character of Orlando from *As You Like It*, who represents gender fluidity and it's an allusion to the hero of Italian writer Ludovico Ariosto's epic poem, *Orlando Furioso,* who, like Woolf's Orlando, is also a poet.

THEMES: Gender and Identity, Nature, Futility of Conformity, Death, Legacy and Fame

PLOT: The adventures of the poet Orlando, who changes his sex from man to woman and lives for centuries, meeting the key figures of English literary history.

MAJOR CHARACTERS: Orlando, aristocratic male-turned female, who lives for centuries and considers poetry above all; **Sasha**, a Russian princess; **Shel,** a sailor whose ambition is to sail around cape; **Nick Greene, Archduke Harry**, who disguises to win the favour of male Orlando.

SETTING: England and the change of sex happens in Constantinople

ADAPTATIONS

- In 1989, the novel has been adapted by the American director Robert Wilson, and writer Darryl Pinckney collaborated on its theatrical production.
- In 1993, it was made into a successful film starring Tilda Swinton as Orlando and Quentin Crisp as Queen Elizabeth I.

SYMBOLS: Oak Tree represents home, **Light and Dark** the light stands for truth and dark is for everything Orlando wants to forget.

QUOTES

"What has praise and fame to do with poetry?"

"They change our view of the world and the world's view of us."

"It was the fatal nature of this disease to substitute a phantom for reality."

POINTS TO REMEMBER

- This novel presents a fictionalised survey of English literature (Dec2013)
- *Orlando* is a biography inspired by Woolf's friend Vita Sackville west

14. Mrs. Dalloway (1925)

AUTHOR: Virginia Woolf

GENRE: Fiction

TITLE: The title refers to the protagonist *Mrs. Dalloway,* whose mind is analysed which receives the myriad expressions of life

THEMES: Age and memory. Passage of time, the after-effects of war, stress and mental illness

PLOT: *Mrs. Dalloway* registers Clarissa Dalloway's 'ordinary mind on an ordinary day' a June day in the life of Clarissa Dalloway, a fictional high-society woman in post–First World War England, who keeps running minor errands in preparation for a party and that is punctuated, and towards the end, by the suicide of a young man she has never met.

MAJOR CHARACTERS: Sir William Bradshaw, a famous Psychiatrist; **Clarissa Dalloway,** 51 year old protagonist; **Elizabeth Dalloway**, Daughter of Mrs Dalloway and Richard; **Richard Dalloway**, husband of Mrs. Dalloway; **MissKilman** a school mistress for history; **Septimus Warren Smith, a** veteran traumatised by his experience in war.

SETTING: The story was set in Wednesday in June 1923 post-World War I London.

ADAPTATIONS :

In 1997, it was adapted into a film by a Dutch film director Marleen Gorris with Eileen Atkins and starred Vanessa Redgrave in the title roles .

SYMBOLS: The Sea the symbol of life, **Flower** is a symbol of love, **Big Ben** represents time and tradition, **Airplanes** represents the impact of war that stays in the mind and life Septimus, **The trees** symbolize the perpetual life force that gives meaning to existence.

QUOTES:

"She always had the feeling that it was very, very dangerous to live even one day."

POINTS TO REMEMBER

- The novel has structural and stylistic similarities to James Joyce's *Ulysses*, it is considered as a response to *Ulysses*.
- ***Clarrisa Dalloway*** is considered as a female Ulysses
- *Mrs Dalloway* fulfils Woolf desire to portray life as " a luminous halo . a semi - transparent envelope surrounding us from the beginning of consciousness to the end"
- It has influenced a lot of works including Michael Cunningham's *"The Hours"* starring Meryl Streep and Nicole Kidman with Kidman playing Woolf

15. Sons and Lovers (1913)

AUTHOR: D.H.Lawrence

GENRE: The Pastoral Novel,The Bildungsroman , autobiographical

TITLE: The title *Sons and Lovers* is very ambiguous, highlights the possibility of woman's son becoming the lover of another woman or an incestuous lover to his mother.

THEMES: Oedipus Complex ,Passion and Love , Bondage

PLOT: The marriage of Gertrude, the mother of the protagonist becomes a battleground with her uneducated and sometimes violent husband Walter Morel, turns her love towards children, especially to William and Paul, her sons. Her dissatisfaction with her social station determined her not to make her sons the coal mines. Gertrude despair gradually develops attachment with her son Paul, who finds it painful to escape his mother's suffocating grasp.

MAJOR CHARACTERS:Paul Morel,The protagonist of the second half of the novel, **Gertrude Morel** , a miserable housewife, **Miriam Leivers**, Paul's best friend, **Clara Dawes**, Paul's lover, **William Morel,** an ambitious student

SETTING: Set in Lawrence's native Nottinghamshire coal mining village of Bestwood

ADAPTATIONS: In 1960 the adapted film version of *Sons and Lovers* won the <u>Academy Award</u>,

SYMBOLS: Swing, symbolizes the vacillating nature of Paul, **Stockings,** represents women's confinement, **Fire,** symbolizes passion

QUOTES:

"She lay as if she had given herself up to sacrifice."

"Love should give a sense of freedom, not of prison."

"I don't think I love you as a man ought to love his wife."

POINTS TO REMEMBER:

- ***Sons and Lovers*** is the first novel with true working class background and also debated as an oedipus novel
- Original title of the novel is **"Paul Morel"**
- The novel contains a frequently quoted use of the English dialect: word "nesh" Nottinghamshire dialect
- D.H Lawrence calls this novel as" one bright book of life"
- "Primitivism" term popularised by D.H. Lawrence through this work
- The last line "He walks towards the faintly glowing town Quickly"(NET) and the novel concludes as Paul Morel Sets off in quest of life away from his mother (June 2016)

16. Women in Love (1920)

AUTHOR: D.H Lawrence

GENRE: Fiction, Romance fiction

TITLE: The title Women in Love is deliberately misleading; the relationships between the two main characters and the men they love are characterized by hatred, anxiety, despair, and violence.

THEMES: Old Way versus New Way, Love and Relationships, Hatred, Violence, and Death

PLOT: The novel tells of the relationships of two sisters, Ursula, a teacher and Gudrun, an artist, who live in a Midland colliery town in pre World War. Ursula falls in love with Birkin and Gudrun's tragic affair with Gerald, the son of a local colliery owner becomes destructive.

MAJOR CHARACTERS: Ursula Brangwen ,Passionate, outspoken school teacher, **Gerald Crich**, the son of a local colliery owner, **Gudrun Brangwen,** an artist with dark desires, **Hermione Roddice**,an eccentric and Pretentious intellectual aristocrat who has an affair with Birkin, **Rupert Birkin** , an intelligent school inspector, who is in search of new values, **Breadalby,**symbolises the sickness of the old way

SETTING: The novel sets in Beldover, a small coal mining town in the Midlands (central part) of England.

ADAPTATIONS: In 1969 the novel was adapted into a film by Larry Kramer under the direction of Ken Russell and it has won Glenda Jackson the Academy Award for Best Actress.

SYMBOLS: Horse, the victimized horse becomes a symbol of unbridled horrors that is devoid of empathy, **Stoning the Moon** ,expresses Rupert rage at a feminine power, **Carpet** suggests the act of smothering and covering.

QUOTES:

> "Instead of chopping yourself down to fit the world, chop the world down to fit yourself."
>
> "One should die quickly, like the Romans, one should be master of one's fate in dying as in living."

REVIEWS/CRITICISM:F. R. Leavis considered it Lawrence's supreme masterpiece.

POINTS TO REMEMBER:

- "An analytical study of sexual depravity" and "an epic of vice" were two of the critical expressions which greeted the publication of "Women in Love"
- Rupert Birkin is the self portrait of D.H.Lawrence
- Lawrence considers the problem in relationships from a philosophical perspective rather than from practical point of view.
- It is a sequel to his earlier novel The Rainbow (1915)

17. The Brave New World (1932)

AUTHOR: Aldous Huxley

GENRE: Dystopian, Science Fiction

TITLE: Brave New World is a phrase taken from Act 5, Scene 1 of *The Tempes*t by William Shakespeare. Miranda, daughter of King Prospero says, "O brave new world, /That has such people isn't."

THEMES: Oppression and Conformity, Identity, Lack of Personal Impact, Consumerism

PLOT: The action of the novel revolves around Bernard Marx, the gloomy Alpha - Plus who pays a visit to New Mexican Reservation and brings savage to England, who is fascinated by the new world and finally revolts to demonstrate the incompatibility of individual freedom and trouble free scientific society.

MAJOR CHARACTERS: John the Savage, the handsome son of the Director and Linda, **Mustapha Mond,** the charismatic leader, **Bernard Marx,** is an alpha - plus male, **Helmholtz Watson**, expert propaganda teacher and creator **Henry Foste**r , alpha-plus genetic engineer, **Lenina Crowne** , obedient beta, lover of Henry, **Linda** , an alpha beta

SETTING: The novel is set in the year A.F 2540 in The cold, sterile Central London Hatchery and Conditioning Center

ADAPTATIONS: In 2015 The Brave New World was adapted into a movie in co-production by Royal &Derngate, and directed by James Dacre.

SYMBOLS: The Letter T, represents the Model T Ford, the first car Henry Ford mass Produced, **Henry Ford,** symbolise materialism and overconsumption, **Decanters**, represents the population of the world state, and **Soma,** represents religion

QUOTES:

"The principle of mass production at last applied to biology."

"Hypnopaedia. The greatest moralizing and socializing force of all time."

"A man can smile and smile and be a villain."

"I ate civilization."

REVIEWS/CRITICISM:

- Rebecca West praised Brave New World as "The most accomplished novel Huxley has yet written",
- Joseph Needham lauded it as "Mr. Huxley's remarkable book",

- Bertrand Russell also praised it, stating, "Mr. Aldous Huxley has shown his usual masterly skill in Brave New World."

POINTS TO REMEMBER:

- Brave New World opens in the year A.F. 632 (after Ford)with the Director of the Central London Hatchery and Conditioning Centre leading a tour of male students through the facility
- The novel is often compared to George Orwell's Nineteen Eighty-Four (1949), who is Huxley's student
- The utopian counterpart of The Brave New World is "Island"
- Describes his experience with India in his travel writing *Jesting Pilate*
- Huxley wrote the introduction to *Bhagavad Gita:The song of God*

18. The Power and The Glory (1940)

_AUTHOR: Graham Greene

GENRE: Christian Fiction

TITLE: The verbally ironic title The Power and the Glory comes from Christian prayer the Lord's Prayer (or Our Father): "For thine is the kingdom and the power and glory, forever and ever, Amen.

THEMES: Suffering, Pride and Piety, Love

PLOT: The action of the novel happens in a poor, remote section of Southern Mexico, where the paramilitary group, the Red Shirts have taken control and God has been outlawed in that region and the priests have been systematically hunted down and killed. The Whisky Priest who is considered to be the last priest is on the run, his compassion for humanity and martyrdom, revives hope.

MAJOR CHARACTERS: Priest, commonly known as whisky Priest, **Lieutenant,** an Indian treated badly in Mexico, **Mestizo,** pursues the priest for money, **Brigitta,** six year old illegitimate daughter of Whisky priest(NET)

SETTING: set in Tabasco in Southern Mexico(NET)

ADAPTATIONS: In 1947, the novel was freely adapted into a film, The Fugitive, directed by John Ford casting Henry Fonda as the priest

The Power and the Glory plays a role in the 2017 short film2048: Nowhere to Run, directed by Luke Scott

SYMBOLS:The Priest, represents the Eucharistic celebration of catholic mass and Jesus, and **Children,** represents future in the novel,

QUOTES:

"Pride was what made the angels fall. Pride's the worst thing of all."

"He felt only an immense disappointment because he had to go to God empty-handed."

"It needed a God to die for the half-hearted and the corrupt."

REVIEWS/CRITICISM: On its publication, William Golding claimed Greene had "captured the conscience of the twentieth century man like no other."

In his introduction, John Updike calls The Power and the Glory, "Graham Greene's masterpiece…. The energy and grandeur of his finest novel derive from the will toward compassion, an ideal communism even more Christian than Communist."

POINTS TO REMEMBER:

- It was initially published in the United States under the title *The Labyrinthine Ways*

- Graham Greene is a Catholic novelist and intelligent officer and a film critic, who sets his novels always in far away places (NET)

- Graham Greene is the friend of R.K.Narayan has appreciated

- and encouraged him to publish his works(NET)

19. A Passage to India (1924)

AUTHOR: E.M Forster (the real name is Henry Morgan)

GENRE: Historical Fiction

TITLE: The title refers to American poet Walt Whitman's poem "A Passage to India." from *Leaves of Grass*. This allusion provides a contrast between Whitman's romantic view of colonization and Forster's darker view of the racism and suppression under the British Raj.

the voyage of Adela Quested from England to India.

THEMES: Failure of Rationality, Colonialism, Human Insignificance, The Inscrutability of India

PLOT: The story is told in three parts involves Aziz,youngmuslim doctor, whose ardor and friendliness with the British swings to hatred and bitterness, When Adela Quested and her elderly companion Mrs Moore arrive in the Indian town of Chandrapore, who longs to explore the 'real India' seek the guidance of Dr Aziz, who organised an expedition to the Marabar caves, where doctor soon finds himself at the centre of a scandal that rouses violent passions among both the British and their Indian subjects. Cultural mistrust and false accusations doom a friendship in British colonial India between an Indian doctor, an Englishwoman engaged to marry a city magistrate, and an English educator.

MAJOR CHARACTERS: Aziz, an young muslim doctor, **Adela,** is a young upper-middle-class Englishwoman, **Mrs. Moore,** Mother of the city magistrate Ronny Heaslop, **Fielding, Principal** at Government college, **Professor Godbole**, Hindu teacher at Government College Hamidullah.

SETTING: Set in India in the city of Chandrapore in British Raj, near Malabar Caves

ADAPTATIONS: The Indian filmmaker Satyajit Ray intended to direct a theatrical adaptation of the novel, but the project was never realised.[18]

SYMBOLS: Caves, symbolise mysteries of both India and the Universe, **Echo,** symbolises the ideal Hindu vision of the world, **Wasp**, represents an object of indiscriminate love.

QUOTES:

"Love in a church, love in a cave, as if there is the least difference."

"Nothing embraces the whole of India, nothing, nothing."

"We exist not in ourselves, but in terms of each other's' minds."

REVIEWS/CRITICISM: Edward Said, renowned critic and literary professor has referenced *A Passage to India* in both *Culture and Imperialism* and *Orientalism*

POINTS TO REMEMBER:

- Forster's connection to India came in the form of a young Indian man named Syed Ross Masood
- A passage to India is the last work of E.M Forster
- Forster visited India in 1921 and worked as a private secretary for another Indian friend, the Maharajah of Dewas
- He dedicated his novel to Syed Ross Masood, who may be the inspiration for the novel's character of Aziz, "and to the 17 years of our friendship"
- Class and connectivity are his favourite THEMES in his novels
- He appreciated Mulkraj Anand for his works
- Central question in the novel is that 'can an Englishman and Indian can be friends?'
- Tom Stoppard reworks E.M Forster A Passage to India as a Cameo in *'Indian Ink'*(NET)
- The novel concludes as 'No not Yet and the sky said no not there' last line (NET)
- E.M.Forster defines novel as "Any fictitious prose work over 50,000words" and as "Novel Tells a Story" in his critical work *Aspects of a Novel*
- Fielding is the mouth piece of EM Forster

20. Oranges are Not the Only Fruit (1985)

AUTHOR: Jeanette Winterson

GENRE: Fiction, Lesbian, Bildungsroman novel

TITLE: The title *Oranges Are Not the Only Fruit* is the statement made by Jeanette's mother towards the end of the novel. It displays the shift in the attitude of the mother towards the end of the novel to accept the daughter

THEMES: Journey to Selfhood, Black-and-White Perception of the world, Importance of Stories

PLOT: This is the story of Jeanette, the adopted child, who was brought up by an evangelist, one of God's elects. Her zealous and passion towards church and religion makes her believe that the girl is destined for life as a missionary, but then she falls for one of her converts. At sixteen, Jeanette decides to leave the church, her home and her family, for the young woman she loves.

MAJOR CHARACTERS: Jeanette, a highly intelligent, repressed and adopted girl, **Jeanette's mother**, a religious, Controlling and uncompromising woman, **zealot Melanie,** friend of Jeanette with whom she has sexual relationship, **Elsie Norris,** Jeanette's friendship with her to grow to maturity, **Miss Jewsbury** , with whom Jeanette maintains a distance, **Katy,** Lover of Jeanette

SETTING: A small town in industrial northern England

ADAPTATIONS: In 1990 BBC adapted this book as a television Drama, starring Charlotte Coleman and Geraldine McEwan, which won the Prix Italia in 1991.

SYMBOLS: Pink Raincoat, represents the mother's pressure on Jeanette to take church centred life, **Walls**, symbolise the constraints in Jeanette's life, **oranges,** represent the black and white perspective of the world, **Pepples,**

QUOTES:

"I loved her because she always knew exactly why things happened"

"If God is your emotional role model, very few human relationships will match up to it."

POINTS TO REMEMBER:

- Postmodern writer writes unconventional and comic novels

- Jeanette fiction has a weak plot structure with no proper beginning, middle and an end. It is a Fragmented narrative with multiple shift in consciousness, chronology and location

- Winterson chooses to structure her semi-autobiographical first novel in eight chapters, each bearing the name of an Old Testament book of the Bible. The chapters of Oranges are Not the Only Fruit are ordered in the same chronology as the old Testament in Bible.

- It has won the Whitbread award.

21.Lucky Jim (1954)

AUTHOR: Sir Kingsley Amis

GENRE: Campus novel (plot revolves around the campus of a university), Satire

TITLE: The novel's title alludes to an old song: "Oh, lucky Jim, / How I envy him. / Oh, lucky Jim. / How I envy him." James "Jim" Dixon is a miserable man for much of the novel. Despite his incompetence and frustrations, he eventually lands the job and the woman of his dreams. This turn of events can only be chalked up to luck.

THEMES: Class Hypocrisy, straightforwardness vs hypocrisy, Luck vs entitlement, Relations between the Sexes, The Sentimentality of Tradition

PLOT: This is the story of Jim Dixon, a lower middleclass lecturer in medieval history at a provincial university who knows better than most that "there was no end to the ways in which nice things are nicer than nasty ones." Dixon struggles to convince **Ned Welch** to continue in the university.

MAJOR CHARACTERS: James Dixon, the titular protagonist, who is history lecturer; bumbles through life, **Christine Callaghan**, an attractive, privileged Londoner, **Ned Welch**, Doddering history department chair **Bertrand Welch,** an amateur and terrible painter **Margaret Peel**, colleague' and lover of James Neurotic female history lecturer, **Bill Atkinson**, ex- molitary man, **Julius Gore-Urquhart**, Wealthy man

SETTING: A university in the English countryside

SYMBOLS: Alcohol, symbolises the escape and abandonment of James from responsibilities and obligations, **"Merrie England"**, symbolizes hypocrisy, boredom, and false conventions, **London**, represents sex

QUOTES:

> "No other professor in Great Britain, he thought, set such store by being called Professor."

> "The tinkle of tiny silver bells."

> "Your attitude measures up to the two requirements of love."

POINTS TO REMEMBER:

- Kinsley Amis dedicated Lucky Jim to his lifelong friend Philip Larkin.
- Lucky Jim is an attack on the forces of boredom
- Kingsley Amis's scabrous debut leads the reader through a gallery of emphatically English bores, cranks, frauds, and neurotics with whom Dixon must contend in one way or another in order to hold on to his cushy academic perch and win the girl of his fancy.

22. Lord of Flies (1954)

AUTHOR: William Golding

GENRE: allegory

TITLE: Golding adopted the title from Milton's *Paradise Lost,* Satan's another version *Beelzebub* which means in Hebrew **Lord of the Flies**, here it refers to a pig's head mounted on a stick by Jack and his band of hunters; it comes to symbolize the potential for evil that resides inside each person.

THEMES: Civilization versus Savagery, Loss of Innocence, Nature of Evil

PLOT: The novel opens with, a plane crashes on an uncharted island, stranding a group of schoolboys under no adult supervision, their freedom is something to celebrate; They attempt to forge their own democratic society, however, they fail in the face of man's nature to terror, sin and evil which eventually collapses all order, as terror begins its reign, the hope of adventure seems as far from reality as the hope of being rescued.

MAJOR CHARACTERS: Ralph, a responsible, reasonable, intelligent, and well socialized boy who tries to bring order, **Jack,**authoritative and dominative leader, **Piggy,** a boy with greater insight and the friend of Ralph,**Simon,** spiritual and humane friend of Ralph , who associated with christ (NET) **Roger,** the Violent and furious boy.

SETTING: Set on a deserted island in the Pacific

ADAPTATIONS: There have been three film adaptations based on the book:

Lord of the Flies (1963), directed by Peter Brook

AlkitrangDugo (1975), a Filipino film, directed by Lupita A. Concio

Lord of the Flies (1990), directed by Harry Hook

SYMBOLS:Piggy's Glasses represents reason and intelligence, **Conch Shell** represents civilization and order, **Pig's Head** represents evil, **War Paint** symbolizes violence, **Uncontrolled Fire** ,represents chaos and evil

QUOTES:

"There aren't any grownups. We shall have to look after ourselves."

"Which is better—to have rules and agree, or to hunt and kill?"

POINTS TO REMEMBER:

- **He was awarded the nobel prize in 1983**
- It is a parable which illustrates his belief that "man produces evil as a bee produces honey"
- World War II and Cold War,these historic conflicts becomes the backdrop for Golding's *Lord of the flies*
- The book's original title *Strangers from Within,* was rejected by the readers for its "too abstract and too explicit"
- Lord of the Flies is perhaps our most memorable novel about "the end of innocence, the darkness of man's heart"

- "Coral Island" by R.M. **B**allantyne is the inspiration for william Golding to write Lord of Flies Ralph and Jack the characters are retained in by Golding (NET)
- 'Life Is Scientific' is a statement often repeated by the character Piggy (NET)

23. *The French Lieutenant's Woman (1969)*

AUTHOR: John Fowles

GENRE: Postmodern historiographic metafiction

TITLE: The title refers to the protagonist Sarah Woodruff, who is also known as The French Lieutenant's Whore

THEMES: Fiction and History Vs. Reality, Storytelling And Morality, Convention Vs. Freedom, Class, Sexuality and Gender Religion, Science, And Evolution

PLOT: The novel explores the fraught relationship of gentleman and amateur naturalist Charles Smithson and Sarah Woodruff, the former governess, an independent woman with whom he falls in love.

MAJOR CHARACTERS: The narrator,**Charles Smithson**, is an upper-class amateur naturalist, **Sarah Woodruff**, the titular French Lieutenant's woman, **Ernestina Freeman** charlesfiancee, **Dr. Grogan**,is an Irish doctor who lives in Lyme. **Sam Farrow**, the Charles's manservant, **Mary**, is a maid at Mrs. Tranter's house.

SETTING: Dorset,Lyme Regis, Exeter, and London, England between 1867 and 1869 the victorian period

ADAPTATIONS: In 1981, the famous playwright Harold Pint**er wrote** the screenplay for its adapted film and it was directed by Karel Reisz

SYMBOLS:Fossils, represents past, **the Brooch** , represents enduring relationship

REVIEWS/CRITICISM:

- The New York Times November 1969 review Lehmann-Haupt found the book to begin as "irresistibly novelistic that he has disguised it as a Victorian romance," yet the metafictional construction by the end positively "explodes all the assumptions of our Victorian sensibilities"

- Roger Sale in The Hudson Review largely criticized the novel, saying, "At times it seems that the commentary is not so bad and the novel awful, but at others Fowles makes the novel almost work and the comments are embarrassingly vulgar

POINTS TO REMEMBER:

- Fowlers stay in a farmhouse in Dorset is the source and base for the Dairy in The French Lieutenant's Woman
- This novel is highly appreciated and highlighted by the critics for its postmodern metafiction which has influenced A. S. Byatt's . Her 1990 Booker Prize-winning novel, Possession is a deliberate response to the model of postmodern metafiction that critics highlight in The French Lieutenant's Woman
- The novel is known for its authorial commentary and has multiple ending as it follows (NET)
  - Charles marries Ernestina

- Charles keeps on searching for Sarah and visits her in D.G.Roosetti as a model she shows the baby
- Sarah is not interested in reviving her relationship so Charles leaves
- After Charles and Sarah argue, Charles perceives that Sarah is offering the opportunity for them to have a platonic relationship. He refuses, and leaves the house without seeing the child

24.*The Prime of Miss Jean Brodi (1961)*

AUTHOR: Muriel Spark, Scottish writer

GENRE: Fiction, female bildungsroman, Psychological Fiction, dystopian

TITLE: The meaning of the title refers to the main character, Miss Jean Brodie. She often tells her students that she is devoted to them "in [her] prime,".

THEMES: The Individual versus the group, Education versus Insight, Conformity versus Nonconformity

PLOT: the novel revolves around the charismatic school teacher Miss Jean Brodie, teacher at Marcia Blaine School for Girls in Edinburgh, Scotland, who is unmistakably, and outspokenly, in her prime. She is passionate about the application of her unorthodox teaching methods and strives to bring out the best in each one of her students and is determined to instill in them independence, passion, and ambition, --but one of them will betray her.

MAJOR CHARACTERS: Miss Brodie, Jean Brodie is a teacher at the Marcia Blaine School for girls, **Sandy Stranger,** Mrs.Brodie's closest confident, **Rose Stanley**, a student **Mr. Lloyd,** Art teacher **Mr. Lowther,** Music teacher

SETTING: Edinburgh Marcia Blaine School

ADAPTATIONS: In 1968 the novel become a play and in 1969 into a film The Prime of Miss Jean Brodie was released. It starred Maggie Smith, and she won the Academy Award for Best Actress for her performance.

SYMBOLS: Portraits, symbolise the unhealthy influence of Miss.Brodie, **The Notebook, symbolises** danger and power of fantasy

QUOTES:

"Give me a girl at an impressionable age, and she is mine for life."

"Art is greater than science."

POINTS TO REMEMBER:

- This novel is considered as a rewriting of Jane Eyre
- The technique used in this novel is prolepsis or flash forward
- Spark was educated in James Gillespie's School for Girls was immortalised in Marcia Blaine School in *The Prime of Miss Jean Brodie*
- The character of Miss Jean Brodie was based in part on Christina Kay, a teacher of Spark's for two years at James Gillespie's School for Girls
- Miss Brodie advises them, "Safety does not come first. Goodness, Truth, and Beauty come first. Follow me"

25. The Sound and Fury (1929)

AUTHOR: William Faulkner, American writer

GENRE: Fiction, Gothic and modernist Fiction.

TITLE: The book's title comes from a famous speech in Shakespeare's Macbeth, describing life as a "tale/Told by an idiot, full of sound and fury, /Signifying nothing."

THEMES: Time,Decay of Family ,Language

PLOT: The novel is about the three Compson brothers' obsessions around the loss of their favourite woman Caddy, the sister.

MAJOR CHARACTERS: Caddy, second of Compson siblings, a strong-willed woman; **Benjy**, the mentally challenged brother of Caddy, **Dilsey**, Strong, compassionate Afro- American lady works for Compson family **Jason**, cruel third son, who is a business failure Quentin**,** oldest son, who commits suicide.

SETTING: The first section of the novel is set in Jefferson, Mississippi, and the second section are set in fictional Yoknapatawpha County, Mississippi, in April 1928

SYMBOLS: Water, symbolises the cleansing of Caddy's affair, **Shadows** represents darkness, **Easter**, symbolizes Christ's death and resurrection, **Quentin's Watch,** represents Quinten's inability to change

QUOTES:

"The broken flower drooped over Ben's fist and his eyes were empty and blue and serene again."

POINTS TO REMEMBER:

- Faulkner decided to create his own fictional world based on Oxford, which he called Yoknapatawpha (pronounced yok-na-pa-TAW-pha) County. It is translated as "water passes slowly through flatlands"

- The novel The **Sound and the Fury** has four parts with different narrator and it opens with Benjy's narration, titled "April Seventh, 1928"

- This book caused in him "the most grief and anguish"

- Faulkner has won the Pulitzer Prize winner in 1955 and 1963

- Faulkner introduces a third person omniscientpoint of view in literarture

- This novel has played a role in William Faulkner's receiving the 1949 Nobel Prize in Literature

26. *The Old Man and the Sea (1952)*

AUTHOR: Ernest Hemingway

GENRE: Novella, Allegory, Bildungsroman, Study guide, Nautical fiction

TITLE: The title refers to the novella's main character, Santiago, an old fisherman, whose struggle with a Marlin, the fish out in the open sea, symbolizing humankind's epic struggle with nature.

THEME: Perseverance, Pain and Suffering, Circle of Life, Pride, Honor, and Respect

PLOT: *The Old Man and the Sea* tells the story of a battle between an aging, experienced fisherman, Santiago, and a large Marlin.

MAJOR CHARACTERS: Santiago, an old fisherman who is considered as an unlucky man. **Manolin**, the young boy who supports and sees Santiago as his mentor, **Marlin**, the 18-foot Marlin, a giant fish is the old man's worthy adversary.

SETTING: The novella was set in Cuba

ADAPTATIONS: *The Old Man and the Sea* has been adapted for the screen three times

- a 1958 film starring Spencer Tracy
- a 1990 miniseries starring Anthony Quinn
- a 1999 animated short film

SYMBOLS: Marlin symbolizes the majestic power of nature, **Joe DiMaggio** represents perseverance and persistence of Santiago, **Mast** is an allusion to cross and in turn symbolizes pain and suffering for a greater good, **Sharks** symbolise the brutal force of destruction, **Manolin** symbolise hope and future.

QUOTES:

"Everything about him was old except his eyes and they ... were cheerful and undefeated."

"He is my brother. But I must kill him and keep strong to do it."

"A man can be destroyed but not defeated."

REVIEWS/CRITICISM:

- Critics have compared *The Old Man and the Sea* with Herman Melville's novel *Moby-Dick.*

POINTS TO REMEMBER:

- In 1953, *The Old Man and the Sea* was awarded the Pulitzer Prize for Fiction, and Hemingway dedicated the award to Cuban people.

- In 1954 Ernest Hemingway was awarded the Nobel prize for literature.

- Hemingway belongs to the group of writers called "Lost Generation"- It's a literary group able to see the disillusionment that the

- Great War brought about.

- Ernest Hemingway says that "All Modern American literature come from one book by Mark Twain called "Adventures of Huckleberry Finn"

27. *A Farewell to Arms (1929)*

AUTHOR: Ernest Hemingway

GENRE: War Literature

TITLE: The novel's title, *A Farewell to Arms*, suggests Henry's farewell to both war (the "arms" of armament) and love (the embracing "arms" of Catherine).

THEME: Disillusionment, Escapism, Chance, Doomed Love, Heartbreak of War.

PLOT: American lieutenant Frederick Henry falls in love with the English nurse Catherine Barkley, who tends to him during his recuperation after he is wounded. She becomes pregnant but refuses to marry him, and he returns to his post. Henry deserts during the Italians' retreat after the Battle of Caporetto, and the reunited couple flees from war to Italy by crossing the border into Switzerland in search of peace. However, it was shattered when Catherine and her baby died during childbirth, leaving Henry desolate.

MAJOR CHARACTERS: Lieutenant Frederic Henry, an American volunteer ambulance driver, **Catherine,** the British nurse and the beloved of Henry, **Rinaldi, a** talented Italian army surgeon

SETTING: Backdrop of World War I, The novel opens in the late autumn of 1916 in the Italian -, Austrian border town of Gorizia.

ADAPTATIONS: In 1996 it was adapted into a film **In Love and War,** directed by Richard Attenborough and starring Chris O'Donnell and Sandra Bullock, which depicts Hemingway's life in Italy as an ambulance driver in the events prior to his writing of *A Farewell to Arms.*

SYMBOLS: Rain is a symbol of doom and **Hair** symbolises isolation and comfort of Henry.

QUOTES:

"I knew I would not be killed. Not in this war. It did not have anything to do with me."

"Tomorrow maybe we drink rainwater."

"It kills the very good and the very gentle and the very brave impartially."

28. *The Great Gatsby (1925)*

AUTHOR: F. Scott Fitzgerald

GENRE: Fiction

TITLE: The title, *The Great Gatsby*, acknowledges Gatsby's great wealth and local

celebrity status but hints at the verbal irony that much of Gatsby's "greatness" is phony.

THEME: Class, Superficiality versus Truth, American Dream, Degradation of Society, American Dream, Degradation of Society

PLOT: The story primarily concerns the young and mysterious millionaire Jay Gatsby, who is a self-made young man whose dream of success is personified in a rich young woman, Daisy Buchanan, who belongs to a corrupt society.

MAJOR CHARACTERS: Jay Gatsby, as a wealthy, charismatic businessman, who has amassed a fortune. **Nick Carraway**, a bright, insightful young man, **Daisy Buchanan**, is a boisterous, unruly, arrogant brute, girlfriend of Jay. **George,** Wilson's garage and gas station operator, **Myrtle Wilson,** Tom's mistress, **Jordan Baker**, Wealthy professional golfer.

SETTING: *The Great Gatsby* is set in 1920s' America i.e, Jazz Age. The Great Gatsby has five settings:

1. The Midwest, from which many of the main characters hail.

2. West Egg, a fictional city on Long Island, New York, where the up-and-coming residents with new money reside.

3. East Egg, a fictional city also on Long Island, where the old aristocratic wealthy people reside.

4. The Valley of Ashes, a third Long Island setting characterized as a bleak locale where the suburbs and less fortunate—the have nots—live.

5. New York, where Nick Carraway works in the bond business and where Tom Buchanan rents an apartment in which he meets with his mistress, Myrtle Wilson.

SYMBOLS: Valley of Ashes symbolises the resident's social status, Green **Light,** symbolise dream, and **The Eyes of Dr. T.J. Eckleburg** symbolises immortality.

QUOTES:

> "Whenever you feel like criticizing anyone, just remember that ... [everyone hasn't] had the advantages that you've had."
>
> "You always look so cool."
>
> "You may fool me but you can't fool God!"

POINTS TO REMEMBER:

- The *The Great Gatsby* concludes as '*So we beat on against the current, borne back ceaselessly into the past*'

- Fitzgerald captures the contradiction of the consumer society through images of automobiles, parties and garbage.

- The novel is narrated by an outsider, Nick Carraway, who was repelled by the tale and his response becomes the subplot. This narrative technique has influenced many.

29. Sister Carrie (1900)

AUTHOR: Theodore Dreiser

GENRE: Fiction

TITLE: Carrie is the nickname of the story's main character, Caroline Meeber. Her family fondly called her "Sister Carrie" when she was young. The title introduces the main character through a relationship.

THEME: Materialism, Morality, The American Dream.

PLOT: The story of a young country girl, Carrie, who moves to the big city, Chicago, where she starts realizing her own American Dream, as a young girl of eighteen she leaves her home. At first, she is a mistress to Drouet and rapidly assumes the cosmopolitan standard of virtue and becomes a famous actress.

MAJOR CHARACTERS: Carrie Meeber, Glamorous, naive young girl **Drouet,** a Charming, fickle young lover of Carrie, **Hurstwood**, a Wealthy and popular old man; **Julia,** a Vindictive, materialistic woman **Minnie,** a Straitlaced, practical woman and sister of Carrie, **Hanson**, Penny-pinching, stern man.

SETTING: The novel was set in Chicago, Montreal, and New York just before the turn of the century, beginning in 1889.

ADAPTATIONS: In 1952, it was adapted into a film starring Laurence Olivier and Jennifer Jones directed by William Wyler.

SYMBOLS: Rocking Chair symbolizes Carrie's emotional and psychological state, **Newspapers** represent Hurston's passive approach to life, **Clothing and Mirrors**, symbolise the importance of physical appearance.

QUOTES:

"A man's fortune ... is very much the same as his bodily growth. Either he is growing stronger, healthier, wiser ... or he is growing weaker, older, less incisive mentally"

POINTS TO REMEMBER:

- Biologist Herbert Spencer (1820–1903), coined the phrase "survival of the fittest."
- Scott Fitzerald, Ernest Hemingway, Dreiser belongs to "Lost Generation" and part of "Jazz Age."
- This novel is the premier example of American naturalism.
- Dreiser's remarkable first novel has deeply influenced such key writers as William Faulkner, F. Scott Fitzgerald, and Saul Bellow.
- *Sister Carrie* is also the greatest of all American urban novels.

<u>30. *Beloved (1987)*</u>

AUTHOR: Toni Morrison

GENRE: Fiction, Magic Realism

TITLE: *Beloved* is the ghost of an infant girl killed by her mother. Her murder is central to all the events in the story. The title is symbolic of all dead and suffering slaves.

THEME: Past versus Present, Loss of Identity in Slavery, Guilt, Love.

PLOT: Sethe, a former slave, who was born as a slave and escaped to Ohio, but even after eighteen years she still feels that she is not free from the memories of Sweet Home, where she was a slave was the beautiful farm where so many hideous things happened. Her new home at 124 Bluestone Road is haunted by the ghost of her baby, whom she killed eighteen years before when she was a slave, because she doesn't want the baby to be a slave. The child has no name and the tombstone is engraved with a single word: Beloved.

MAJOR CHARACTERS: Sethe, an escaped slave, is the main character of the novel, **Beloved**, baby killed by the mother and haunts the family, **Denver**, Sethe's youngest child, is an innocent victim of the family, **Paul D**, a fellow slave, **Baby Suggs**, Sethe's mother-in –law.

SETTING: The setting is the outskirts of Cincinnati, Ohio, in 1873.

ADAPTATIONS:

- In 1998 ***Beloved*** was adapted into a movie of the same name starring Oprah Winfrey.

SYMBOLS: Colors represents different things for characters, **Water** symbolises escape from slavery, **Trees** represents comfort and evil, **124** represents the house and also represents her children, **Baby Ghost** represents horrors and slavery.

QUOTES:

"Anything dead coming back to life hurts."

"The pieces I am, she gathers them and give them back to me in all the right order."

"We got more yesterday than anybody. We need some kind of tomorrow."

POINTS TO REMEMBER:

- ***Beloved*** is inspired by the true story of Margaret Garner. Born a slave in Kentucky, Garner, her husband, and their four children escaped to Cincinnati in 1856.
- Toni Morrison has stated that the purpose of ***Beloved*** is 'to fill in the blanks that the slave narrative left, to part the veil that was so frequently drawn'
- The First Afro - American woman to be awarded the Nobel prize in 1993
- The novel won the Pulitzer Prize for Fiction in 1988

- The narrative technique used in this novel is non-linear and complex.
- The book's epigraph *"I will call them my people, which were not my people; and her beloved, which was not beloved.* is taken from the Bible, Romans 9:25.
- Toni Morrison dedicated this book to 'Sixty Million and More'

31. *Their Eyes were Watching God (1937)*

AUTHOR: Zora Neale Hurston

GENRE: Bildungsroman or coming-of-age story

TITLE: The title *Their Eyes Were Watching God* comes from a sentence in Chapter 18: "They seemed to be staring at the dark, but their eyes were watching God." The narrator makes the statement during a hurricane.

THEME: Love, Independence, Gender roles, Race, Judgment.

PLOT: The plot revolves around the protagonist Janie Crawford, a Fair and long-legged, independent and articulate woman, whose quest for selfhood makes her set out of her house to be her own person -- no mean feat for a black woman in the '30s. Janie's quest for identity takes her through three marriages and into a journey back to her roots.

MAJOR CHARACTERS: Janie Crawford, a resilient, strong willed woman, **Pheoby**, a friend of Janie, **Nanny**, former slave and grandmother of Janie, **Logan Killicks, Joe Starks** an ambitious businessman **Tea Cake**, a gambler and musician, Janie's true love.

SETTING: *Their Eyes Were Watching God* is set in the early 20th century in Florida during the era of strict racial segregation laws.

ADAPTATIONS: In 2011, the novel was adapted as a radio play for BBC World Drama, dramatized by Patricia Cumper. The play first aired on February 19, 2011.

SYMBOLS: Pear Tree, a symbol of change and growth, **Gate** represents limitations and safety, **Head Rag and Janie's Hair** represent suppression and control, **The mule** symbolizes mistreatment and cruelty, **The horizon and the road** are powerful symbols of freedom and opportunity.

QUOTES:

"Ships at a distance have every man's wish on board."

"Honey, de white man is de ruler of everything."

"Here was peace. She pulled in her horizon like a great fish-net."

POINTS TO REMEMBER:

- This novel has been regarded as a seminal work in both African-American literature and women's literature and a critique of Southern African-American folk society.
- Alice Walker had her headstone inscribed "Zora Neale Hurston: The Genius of the South"
- The novel is criticised for its vernacular speech and spelling
- Janie finishes telling her story to Pheoby, saying she has "been tuh de horizon and back."

Zora Neale Hurston is very prominent in Harlem Renaissance

<u>*32. The Colour Purple (1982)*</u>

AUTHOR: Alice Walker.

GENRE: Epistolary novel; the 20th-century African-American.

TITLE: Through the word color purple Alice Walker is presenting the independence and liberation of one's mind and feelings. Shug used this term in the novel to Celia, she says: "I think it pisses God off if you walk by the color purple in a field somewhere and don't notice it."

THEME: God and Spirituality, Race and Racism, Men, Women and Gender Roles, Violence and Suffering, Self-Discovery

PLOT: *The Colour Purple* shows what happens to a young black woman Celie, born into poverty and segregation. She had a disastrous life: she was raped repeatedly by the man she calls 'father', she has two children taken away from her and killed by her father, and also she is separated from her beloved sister Nettie. She is trapped into an ugly marriage to an old man she despises. However, her life turns when she meets the glamorous Shug Avery, singer and magic-maker - a woman who has taken charge of her own destiny. Gradually, Celie discovers the power and joy of her own spirit, freeing herself from her past and reuniting herself with those she loves.

MAJOR CHARACTERS: Celie, the novel's protagonist, **Nettie,**Celie's more attractive younger sister. **Mr.Albert,** abusive husband who hurts celie, **Shug Avery,** a singer, **Sofia**,a strong-minded and physically strong woman, and the first wife of Harpo.

SETTING: The novel was set in Georgia and coastal Africa, roughly around 1920-1950.

ADAPTATIONS: In 1985, the novel was adapted into a film *The Color Purple*, directed by Stephen Spielberg, a white, male filmmaker.

On December 1, 2005, a musical adaptation of the novel (based on the film) opened at The Broadway Theatre in New York City

SYMBOLS: PURPLE, the colour purple symbolises love, **Pants** represents the transformation of Celie into an independent woman, **GOD** represents salvation.

QUOTES: "Dear God, I am fourteen years old. I am I have always been a good girl. Maybe you can give me a sign letting me know what is happening to me."

POINTS TO REMEMBER:

- *The Color Purple* won the Pulitzer Prize for Fiction in 1983,
- The whole novel was narrated through letters from Celie to God and to and from her sister Nettie

<u>*33. Invisible Man (1952)*</u>

AUTHOR: Ralph Ellison

GENRE: Fiction, Bildungsroman

TITLE: The title *Invisible Man* highlights the narrator's central struggle of feeling invisible in a white culture dominated society.

THEME: Invisibility, Slavery's Baggage, Racial Expectations.

PLOT: *Invisible Man* is a claustrophobic novel where the protagonist journeys from the Deep South to the streets and basements of Harlem in quest of identity, a horrifying "battle royal" where black men are reduced to fighting animals, to a Communist rally where they are elevated to the status of trophies, Ralph Ellison's nameless protagonist ushers' readers into a parallel universe that throws our own into harsh and even hilarious relief.

MAJOR CHARACTERS: Narrator is a young, light-skinned black man who becomes disillusioned in his quest to create a unique identity, **Dr. Bledsoe,** subservient to whites, **Mr. Norton** is a wealthy, white trustee of the black college Trueblood, **Brother Jack** is the white leader of the Brotherhood in Harlem.

SETTING: The novel was set in America's South during the late 1920s to early 1930s.

SYMBOLS: Liberty Paints symbolically covers blackness in the same way that the narrator's education sought to hide his black heritage, or culture, **The Sambo Doll** symbolises a subservient, lazy slave, **Mary's Bank** symbolise narrator's identity, **Vision,**

symbolic of their varying inabilities to recognize the narrator's struggles.

QUOTES:

"I am an invisible man. ... I am invisible, understand, simply because people refuse to see me."

"We are the machines inside the machine."

"By pretending to agree I had indeed agreed."

POINTS TO REMEMBER:

- This book is categorized as a bildungsroman because the novel focuses on the narrator's formative years or spiritual awakening and growth.
- The book has won the National Book Award.
- The book challenges readers with its jazz music style, swaying between harsh realism and dreamlike fantasy.
- The former U.S. president Barack Obama modeled his memoir: ***Dreams from My Father*** on Ellison's novel.
- *Invisible Man* is one of those rare novels that has changed the shape of American literature and is dedicated to the richness of life and art that becomes possible when the imagination is liberated from close realism.
- "If the Negro, or any other writer, is going to do what's expected of him, he's lost the battle before he takes the field" - remark by Ralph Ellison serves as a motto to his career

34. *Wide Sargasso Sea (1966)*

_**AUTHOR:** Jean Rhys

GENRE: Romantic novel, Historical Fiction, Postmodern novel, Parallel novel

TITLE: The title *Wide Sargasso Sea* refers to a windless area in the northern Atlantic Ocean where ships get entangled in masses of seaweed. The title is a metaphor for the characters, who are also trapped in real or perhaps imagined ways between countries and racial heritages.

THEME: Women and Power, Alienation and Identity, Slavery and Entrapment

PLOT: This novel *Wide Sargasso Sea* describes the life and marriage of Antoinette Cosway, a creole heiress, a sensual and protected young woman who is sold into marriage to the prideful Mr. Rochester. Cosway amidst a society so driven by hatred, so skewed in its sexual relations drive her out of her mind and mad.

MAJOR CHARACTERS: Antoinette Cosway, the protagonist, **Rochester,** marries Antoinette for wealth, **Christophine**, Annette is an emotional woman, **Destitute widow**, goes mad after her son's death, **Mr. Mason**, Rich British man.

SETTING: *Wide Sargasso Sea* is set in Dominica and post-emancipated Jamaica in 1830s.

ADAPTATIONS:

- In 2011 Stevie Nicks, rock 'n' roll singer wrote a song "Wide Sargasso Sea" and included in her album, *In Your Dreams*, about the novel

SYMBOLS: Garden symbolises seclusion of the protagonist, **Fire** represents destruction, **Forest** is symbolic of a place of life, death, decay and growth, sustenance and beauty.

QUOTES:

"Have all beautiful things sad destinies?"

"There is no looking glass here and I don't know what I am like now."

POINTS TO REMEMBER:

- Inspiration for *Wide Sargasso Sea* was Charlotte Brontë's *Jane Eyre*, in which the character Bertha Mason appeared.
- *Wide Sargasso Sea* is both a response and a prequel to Charlotte Brontë's *Jane Eyre*, set in the West Indies and imagining the lives of Bertha Mason and her family.
- Rhys brings back her Caribbean childhood.

35.*Never Let Me Go (2005)*

AUTHOR: Kazuo Ishiguru

GENRE: Dystopian, Science Fiction

TITLE: The title *Never Let Me Go* is the name of Kathy's favorite song on a cassette tape called "Songs After Dark" by Judy Bridgewater.

THEME: Inevitable Loss and Death, Human Clones Are Not Machines, No One Can Take Away Memories, Nature versus Nurture

PLOT: It is the story of kathy's transformation from a small school girl in Hailsham (a pleasant English boarding school far from the influences of the city), who is trained in art and literature but nothing about the outside world. Kathy encounters the realities of the world only when she and her friends, Ruth and Tommy, leave the safe grounds of the school, that they realize the reality of her school.

MAJOR CHARACTERS: Kathy, an Introspective decisive woman, the protagonist and narrator, **Tommy**, an athletic and highly sensitive friend of Kathy. **Ruth**, the unpredictable, controlling, and manipulative, **Madame**, a woman who visits Hailsham to pick up the children's artwork, whose name is Marie-Claude, **Miss Emily,** Headmistress of Hailsham, **Miss Lucy** is a young athlete.

SETTING: The novel is set in England in the 1990s.

ADAPTATIONS:

- Mark Romanek directed a British film adaptation titled **Never Let Me Go** in 2010.
- In 2016 a Japanese television aired this drama.

SYMBOLS: "Never Let Me Go" and the Cassette Tape, Tommy's Drawings represent the complicated and intricate, carefully crafted expression of Tommy. **Hailsham** symbolizes the idea that *clones are human beings*.

QUOTES:

"Memories, even your most precious ones, fade surprisingly quickly. But I don't go along with that. The memories I value most, I don't ever see them fading."

"All children have to be deceived if they are to grow up without trauma."

POINTS TO REMEMBER:

- Ishiguro won the Nobel Prize in Literature in 2017.

36. *Midnight's Children (1981)*

AUTHOR: Salman Rushdie

GENRE: Postcolonial and postmodern novel, Magical Realism (a specific type of artistic realism that attempts to portray everyday occurrences filled with magical or supernatural elements).

TITLE: The title of Salman Rushdie's novel *Midnight's Children* refers to "1001" children that are born just at midnight as it strikes the dawn of India's Independence, i.e. 15 August 1947. It is believed that all these children have magical/superpowers.

THEME: Truth and Storytelling, British Colonialism and Postcolonialism, Sex and Gender, Identity and Nationality.

PLOT: Salman Rushdie is an epic novel that opens up with a child being born at midnight on 15 August 1947, the novel begins with the story of Sinai's family and the various events that lead to India's independence and eventually to partition. Born precisely at midnight, Saleem was born with telepathic powers and later discovers that all the kids born in India between 12 A.M. and 1 A.M. are impregnated with the special power.

MAJOR CHARACTERS: Saleem Sinai, the protagonist and narrator, **Shiva,** the story's antagonist and Saleem Sinai's alter ego. **Aadam Aziz,** Saleem Sinai's grandfather.

SETTING: The novel is set in Independent India.

ADAPTATIONS: In 2003, the novel was adapted as a stage show by the Royal Shakespeare Company.

SYMBOLS: Noses, Saleem Sinai's large, bulbous nose is a symbol of his power as the leader, **Pickles** is a phallic symbol, **Spittoons** symbolise Saleem's identity.

QUOTES:

"What's real and what's true aren't necessarily the same."

"We all owe death a life."

"Most of what matters in our lives takes place in our absence."

"What can't be cured must be endured."

POINTS TO REMEMBER:

- One of the most important historical events in *The Midnight's Children* is Indira Gandhi's Emergency, a country-wide state of emergency.

- *The Midnight's Children* won both the Booker Prize and the James Tait Black Memorial Prize in 1981. It was awarded the "Booker of Bookers" Prize and the best all-time prize winners in 1993 and 2008.

- In 1984, Prime Minister Indira Gandhi brought an action against the book in the British courts, claiming to have been defamed by a single sentence in chapter 28, penultimate paragraph, in which her son Sanjay Gandhi is said to have accused her mother to have contributed to the death of his father Feroze Gandhi's death through her neglect. The case was settled out of court when Salman Rushdie agreed to remove the offending sentence.

37.A House for Mr Biswas (1961)

AUTHOR: V.S.Naipaul

GENRE: Tragic-comedy fiction

TITLE: The title *A House for Mr Biswas* **refers** to Mr. Biswas desire to own a house of his own, to assert and preserve his independence.

THEME: Independence vs. Belonging, Social Status and Hierarchy, Education, Work, and Language, Gender and Family.

PLOT: It is a tragic tale of the protagonist, Mohun Biswas, who has spent 46 years of life striving for independence. He has shuttled from one residence to another in his life after the drowning of his father, he yearns for a place he can call his home. He marries into the Tulsi family, where he becomes a dependent, but rebels and takes on a succession of occupations in a struggle to weaken their hold over him.

MAJOR CHARACTERS: Mr Mohun Biswas, the protagonist, is a cynical Indo-Trinidadian man, **Shama,** Mr Biswas' wife, **Savi**, Mr Biswas' eldest daughter, **Anand,** Mr Biswas` son.

SETTING: The novel is set in Trinidad in the first half of the twentieth century.

SYMBOLS: House symbolises the self-identity of Mr.Biswas, **Barracks** represents the confinement of life, **Hanuman House** symbolises traditionalism, rigidity and cultural perfection.

QUOTES: "But life is like that. Is not a fairy story."

REVIEWS/CRITICISM:

A work of great comic power qualified with firm and unsentimental comparrison - Anthony Burges.

POINTS TO REMEMBER:

- Booker prize for *In a Free State* in 1971 and he was awarded the Nobel Prize in 2001.
- Echoes of Shakespeare's *King Lear* is felt in the novel.

38. *Half of a Yellow Sun (2006)*

AUTHOR: Chimamanda Ngozi Adichie

GENRE: Historical fiction

TITLE: The title represents the Biafran flag, which features an image of half of a yellow sun set against three horizontal stripes—red, black, and green. The sun rising symbolizes tenacity and hope for a future of self-determination against great odds.

THEME: Navigating Postcolonial Identity, Racism and Ethinic Identity.

PLOT: The novel portrays the realities and horrors of Biafra war through his characters Ugwa, a house boy in the professor Odenigbo house and Olanna, the mistress of the professor and her twin sister, Kainene, and Richard, the shy young Englishman. Chimamanda Ngozi Adichie weaves together the lives of three characters swept up in the turbulence of the decade. The turbulence of War has dynamic changes in the life that tear their lives apart which made them run for their lives. The War becomes a great threat to their ideals and loyalties to one another.

MAJOR CHARACTERS: Ugwu, a houseboy turned writer, **Olanna,** the professor's mistress who is known for her beauty, kindness, and empathy, **Richard,** a journalist who has come to Nigeria, **Kainene** is Olanna's twin sister, less beautiful but confident, independent and fearless, **Odenigbo** is a professor of mathematics, a socialist, a tribalist.

SETTING: The novel is set in Nigeria during the Nigerian Civil War.

ADAPTATIONS:

In 2013, a film adaptation of the novel written by playwright Biyi Bandele premiered at the Toronto International Film Festival and had its worldwide release in 2014.

SYMBOLS: Girl's Head in Calabash, the most poignant and potent symbol that symbolises the horrors of war. It also symbolizes the end of normalcy. **Half of a Yellow Sun**, the official symbol of Biafra.

QUOTES:

"My life will change only if I want it to change."

"When I lost the whole family ... it was as if I had been born all over again."

"He was not living his life; life was living him."

"The white man brought racism into the world. He used it ... to conquer a more humane people."

REVIEWS/CRITICISM:

- The Great Nigerian writer Chinua Achebe cheers: "We do not usually associate wisdom with beginners, but here is a new writer endowed with the gift of ancient storytellers," and said about Adichie: "She is fearless, or she would not have taken on the intimidating horror of Nigeria's civil war."

- **The Washington Post Book World** acclaimed Adichie as "the 21st-century daughter of Chinua Achebe."

- Maya Jaggi called the second novel of Chimamanda second novel as "a landmark novel" *The Guardian*.

POINTS TO REMEMBER:

- The novel was awarded the Baileys Women's Prize for Fiction in 2007.

- Her first novel is **Purple Hibiscus (2003)** is the exploration of Nigerian Family.

- **Half of a Yellow Sun** re-creates a seminal moment in modern African history: Biafra's impassioned struggle to establish an independent republic in Nigeria in the 1960s.

- The novel ends in ambiguity and the readers are not informed what happened to Kainene

39. Things Fall Apart (1958)

AUTHOR: Chinua Achebe

GENRE: Historical fiction

TITLE: The title *Things Fall Apart* is taken from the Irish poet William Butler Yeats's poem "The Second Coming". The novel resonates the woeful plight of the post World War I.

THEME: Culture and Change, Fate versus Free Will, Betrayal.

PLOT: The novel chronicles the life of Okonkwo, the "strong man", the leader of an Igbo community, whose life is dominated by fear and anger which ends up in exile for seven years from his own community for accidentally killing a clansman. The novel gives a special focus into the intrusion of white missionaries and colonial government into tribal Igbo society in 1980. Thus it talks about the problems of Africa and simultaneous disintegration of its protagonist Okonkwo and of his village.

MAJOR CHARACTERS: Okonkwo, a man who values masculinity, strength, and respect, **Unoka**, a lazy but gifted musician and gentleman in the clan, **Ikemefuna**, boy who comes for payment but decides to live with Oknokwo, **Nwoye**, Son of Okonkwo who rebels and leaves the house, **Ekwefi**, Okonkwo's second wife, **Ezinma**, the only child of Okonkwo's second wife, **Obierika**, the bosom friend of Okonkwo.

SETTING: *Things Fall Apart* takes place in the fictional place called **Iguedo** in 1890s in Igbo villages in Nigeria.

ADAPTATIONS: In April 1961, the book was adapted radio drama called **Okonkwo** by the Nigerian Broadcasting Corporation, where Wole Soyinka acts as a minor character.

SYMBOLS: Fire represents Okonkwo's rage and combustible nature. **Yams** grown by Igbo men as a symbol of masculinity, **The Locusts** represent the arrival of the white man and missionaries.

QUOTES:

> "Never kill a man who says nothing."

> "He had already chosen the title ... The Pacification of the Primitive Tribes of the Lower Niger."

> "Living fire begets cold, impotent ash."

REVIEWS/CRITICISM: Hilary Mantel, the Booker Prize-winning novelist in a 7 May 2012 article in The Newsweek, lists **Things Fall Apart** as one of her five favourite novels in the genre of Historical Fiction.

POINTS TO REMEMBER:

- *Things Fall Apart* is the debut novel of Chinua Achebe.

- **In 1960,** Achebe came up with *No Longer at Ease*, a sequel to *Things Fall Apart.*

- *Af*rican author **Nadine Gordimer**, dubbed Achebe the ***"father of modern African literature,"*** an unofficial title by which he commonly became known.

- It is seen as the archetypal modern African novel in English.

40. Disgrace (1999)

AUTHOR: J.M. (John Maxwell) Coetzee

GENRE: Fiction

TITLE: The title attributes to the social and spiritual disgrace of the Protagonist and professor David Lurie owing to his affair with one of his students.

THEME: Disgrace, The Problem of Sex, Challenges of Aging, changing country, subjugation of woman.

PLOT: This searing novel spins around the protagonist David Lurie, a twice divorced, 52-year-old professor of Communications and Romantic Poetry at Cape Technical University. He lives a comfortable and passionless life for himself within his financial and emotional means. He loses everything because of his sexual activity especially when Lurie seduces one of his students Melanie Isaacs that sets in motion a chain of events that shatters his complacency and leaves him utterly disgraced.

MAJOR CHARACTERS: David Lurie, is a stubborn and proud Professor. **Melanie Isaacs,** the seduced student, **Lucy Lurie,** the mature, practical, and responsible daughter of Lurie, **Petrus**, a middle-aged black man belonging to the Xhosa people.

SETTING: The novel is set in post-apartheid South Africa shortly after the end of apartheid, in the rural Eastern Cape near Grahamstown.

ADAPTATIONS: A film adaptation of *Disgrace* won the International Critics' Award at its world premiere at the Toronto International Film Festival in 2008.

SYMBOLS: David's Opera, the opera symbolizes David's feelings, desires, and circumstances throughout the plot. **Animals** symbolise the human tendency to subjugate.

QUOTES:

> "They do us the honor of treating us like gods, and we respond by treating them like things."

> "If he is being led, then what god is doing the leading?"

POINTS TO REMEMBER:

- The technique of free, indirect discourse is used in *Disgrace*, where the narrator reveals the protagonist David Lurie's thoughts and interior perspectives.

- A significant part of the intertextuality in *Disgrace* is the text's dialogue with the works, ideas, and lives of two English Romantic poets: William Wordsworth and Lord Byron.

- In 2003, he was awarded the Nobel Prize for Literature four years after the publication of *Disgrace*.

- Lurie's confront the ignorance at the aging both at the individual and at societal level, which alludes to the line, "No country, this, for old men," an ironic reference to the opening line of the W. B. Yeats' poem, "*Sailing to Byzantium*".

41. *The English Patient (1992)*

AUTHOR: Michael Ondaatje

GENRE: Historic Metafiction, a term coined by Canadian literary theorist Linda Hutcheon in 1980s which includes the domains of Fiction, History, and Theory.

TITLE: The title, *The English Patient*, refers to the nickname of the main character—a burn victim whose identity is erased by his injuries, as well as by his desire for anonymity.

THEME: Intertextuality, Destructiveness of War, Identity, Race, Ethnicity, and Nationality

PLOT: The novel traces the intersection of four damaged lives, the eponymous patient considered English, Hana, the exhausted Canadian army nurse; Caravaggio, the maimed Canadian thief; Kip, a Sikh British Army sapper in an Italian villa at the end of World War II. All the four characters are haunted by the riddle of the English patient, the nameless, burned man who lies in an upstairs room and whose memories of passion, betrayal, and rescue illuminate this book like flashes of heat lightning. The novel ends with Kip learning that the U.S. has bombed Hiroshima and Nagasaki. The novel concludes as Kip leaves the Villa, San Girolamo, learning that the U.S. has bombed Hiroshima and Nagasaki.

MAJOR CHARACTERS: The English patient, is a well-read, educated Hungarian count by the name of Ladislaus de Almásy; **Caravaggio,** a Canadian thief who uses his skills to become a spy;**Hana,** is a nurse, originally from Canada; **Kip,** alias**Kirpal Singh**, an Indian by birth, a young soldier who is trained to disarm explosives.

SETTING: The novel *The English Patient* is set in a damaged Villa, San Girolamo, in Tuscany, a region in west- central Italy. The portion of the novel that describes the English patient's past is set mostly in the Sahara, the world's largest desert, North Africa.

ADAPTATIONS: In 1996, the novel was adapted into a film which received nine Academy Awards including Best Picture and Director at the 69th Academy Awards.

SYMBOLS: Bombs represent the tremendous capacity of human intelligence of evil, **the Villa** symbolizes the destruction of the war on the main characters, **Kip's Turban** represents difference, **Books** symbolise a way forward for Hana.

QUOTES:

"You have to protect yourself from sadness. Sadness is very close to hate."

"You must consider the character of your enemy. This is true of bomb disposal."

"She had always wanted words, she loved them; grew up on them. Words gave her clarity, brought reason, shape."

Dr.SHERLIN SMILE

"All I ever wanted was a world without maps."

"A novel is a mirror walking down a road."

POINTS TO REMEMBER:

- Although *The English Patient*(1992) is not strictly a sequel to *In the Skin of a Lion* (1987), Ondaatje extends the stories of several characters from his earlier novel here.
- The Book won the 1992 Booker Prize and The Golden Man Booker in 2018, and the Governor General's Award.

42. *The Handmaid's Tale (1985)*

AUTHOR: Margaret Atwood

GENRE: Dystopian, Speculative Fiction, Science Fiction, Dystopian Fiction, Feminist Science Fiction

TITLE: The narrator is one of a class of women known as Handmaids, women who serve as birth mothers for childless elites. The novel's title echoes the component parts of Geoffrey Chaucer's *The Canterbury Tales*, which is a series of connected stories ("The Merchant's Tale", "The Parson's Tale", etc.)

THEME: Identity, Language, Gender Roles, Liberty and Captivity

PLOT: The novel focuses on the journey of the handmaid Offred. Offred is a Handmaid in the Republic of Gilead, a totalitarian and theocratic state that has replaced the United States of America, where the failing fertility leads to the enslavement of women for breeding purpose. Offred is one such girl who is enslaved for the same purpose, she tells the story of her daily life, where she frequently slips into flashbacks, from which the reader can reconstruct the events leading up to the beginning of the novel.

MAJOR CHARACTERS: Offred, the narrator whose real name is unknown; **The Commander**, one who leads the government; **Serena Joy**, a former religious television personality and anti-feminist speaker; **Nick, As a Guard**—a low-level servant; **Moira**, another handmaid like Offred.

SETTING: Novel is set in what once was the Harvard Square close to Cambridge, Massachusetts in the imaginary Republic of Gilead, formerly the United States.

ADAPTATIONS: In 1990,Harold Pinter wrote the screenplay for the film version of *The Handmaid's Tale* which was directed by Volker Schlöndorff.

 SYMBOLS: Red, the color of blood, represents the role of the Handmaids; **The Eyes of God** are the secret police of Gilead, and they use winged eyes as their symbol; **Flowers** symbolize fertility and reproduction.

QUOTES:

> "It was true, I took too much for granted; I trusted fate, back then."
>
> "There's always a black market, there's always something that can be exchanged."
>
> "Better never means better for everyone ... It always means worse, for some."

POINTS TO REMEMBER:

- This novel is dedicated to Mary Webster about whom Atwood also wrote the poem "Half-Hanged Mary." Webster, an American puritan ancestor of Atwood.

- The novel is best known for its double narrative: Offred's narrative and Handmaid's narrative.

- The novel concludes with metafictional epilogue, the term 'metafiction' was coined in 1970 by William H. Gass in his book *Fiction and the Figures of Life*.

- Atwood published the sequel novel, *The Testaments*, in 2019.

43. Surfacing (1972)

AUTHOR: Margaret Atwood

GENRE: Domestic Fiction

TITLE: The title refers to the unnamed protagonist, who brings her distressed and suppressed memories to the surface of her conscious mind like something emerging from the deep lake to its surface.

THEME: Separation versus Wholeness, Power, Natural versus Artificial

PLOT: The book revolves around the unnamed protagonist, a talented artist, who along with her friends and lover returns to her hometown in Canada in search of her missing father on a remote island in Northern Quebec. Her childhood house evokes more events and feelings. Gradually, the past overtakes her and drives her into the realm of wildness and madness in the isolated setting.

MAJOR CHARACTERS: The **unnamed protagonist**, an artist; **David,** friend, a selfish and abusive exploiter;**Joe,**the lover; **Anna,** a shallow, catty manipulator and spouse of David.

SETTING: Quebec,Canada

ADAPTATIONS: It was adapted into a movie in 1981.

SYMBOLS: Surfacing is a metaphor to symbolise the emotional journey of the narrator to her past. **Water**symbolizes the narrator's subconscious. **Dead Hero** symbolizes the passive victimhood of Canadian culture. **Barometer Couple** is a symbol of the forces that keep relationships together. **Americans**symbolize commercialization.

QUOTES:

"A divorce is like an amputation, you survive but there's less of you."

"Nothing is the same, I don't know the way anymore."

"The barometer couple ... my ideal; except they were glued there ... without escape."

"This above all, to refuse to be a victim."

POINTS TO REMEMBER:

- Sylvia Plath's only novel,*The Bell Jar,*is often compared to Atwood's *Surfacing*. For, the protagonists, Atwood's unnamed narrator and Plath's Esther Greenwood face psychological breakdowns due to their unwillingness to adhere to the social expectations imposed on women.
- The structure of *Surfacing* parallels with the structure of Jack Kerouac's *On the Road* , where the protagonist travels to her childhood home by car.

44. *One Hundred Years of Solitude (1967)*

AUTHOR: Gabriel García Márquez, Caribbean Writer

GENRE: Tragi-comic novel, Family saga, Epic fiction

TITLE: The title, *One Hundred Years of Solitude*, refers to the change and emotional isolation that stumble upon the characters at the fictional town of Macondo in Colombia in a century.

THEME: Love, Past and Present, Complexity of Time, Incest, and Solitude

PLOT: The novel is an epic tale of seven generations of the Buendía family for a century, from the postcolonial 1820s to the 1920s. It chronicles the characters' thirst for love and the irreconcilable conflict between the desires for solitude.

MAJOR CHARACTERS: José ArcadioBuendía, the patriarch of the Buendía family and the founder of Macondo, Stubborn and ambitious, marries his cousin; **Ursula,** a strong clairvoyant who lives a full 100 years to see all seven generations; **Colonel AurelianoBuendía,** José ArcadioBuendía's second son and the first person to be born in Macondo; **Melquíades,** a gypsy who visits Marcondo every March; **Amaranta Buendía**, the youngest child and only daughter in the second generation.

SETTING: The novel is set in Macondo, a fictional town of the author.

ADAPTATIONS: On March 6, 2019, GarcíaMárquez's son Rodrigo GarcíaBarcha, announced that Netflix was developing a series based upon the book set to release in 2020.

SYMBOLS: Macondo representsColombia's controversial history of civil wars, colonialism, plantation economy, and industrialization.**The railroad** a symbol representing Macondo's evolution from village.**Yellow and Gold** are symbols of the Spanish Golden Age and imperialism. **Ghost** symbolizes the haunting nature of past.**Glass city** represents the fate of Buendia.

QUOTES:

"Everything is known."

"Children inherit their parents' madness"

REVIEWS/CRITICISM:

"The first piece of lit since the Book of Genesis that should be required reading for the entire human race." - KennedyNew York Times

Chilea Poet Laureate Pablo Neruda called it "The greatest revelation in the Spanish language since Don Quixote of Cervantes."

POINTS TO REMEMBER:

- *Hundred years of Solitude* is a tragicomic novel of magic realism. It's the Magnum opus of Garcia Marquez and has left a marked influence in Spanish literary canon.

- Magic realism is first experimented by the Cuban Novelist **Alegio Carpentier** and he called it *Marvellous Realism.*

- Melquíades has been revealed as the narrator by the end of the novel.

- Originally, *One Hundred Years of Solitude*, formerly titled "The House" and was published in Spanish.

- The book was translated into English by Gregory Rabassa.

- In 1982 GarcíaMárquez won the Nobel Prize in Literature.

- The phrase **"Many Years Later"** repeated 9 times in English translation and "Later" for 83 times.

<u>*45. Lolita (1955)*</u>

AUTHOR: Vladimir Nabokov - Russian American writer

GENRE: Fiction, Tragi-comedy, Erotic literature

TITLE: "Lolita" is the nickname the narrator gives to the 12-year-old girl Dolores Haze, with whom he is obsessed.

THEME: Pathological Misogyny, Power, Aesthetics, Time, and Memory

PLOT: The plot revolves around Humbert Humbert - scholar, aesthete and romantic fallen blindly in love with Lolita Haze, his landlady's gum-snapping, silky skinned twelve-year-old daughter. He marries Mrs.Haze reluctantly just to be close to Lolita, Humbert suffers greatly in the pursuit of romance; but when Lo herself starts looking for attention elsewhere, he will carry her off on a desperate cross-country misadventure, all in the name of Love.

MAJOR CHARACTERS:Humbert Humbert, is a European intellectual; **Dolores Haze** nicknamed as **Lolita**; a lively innocent 12-year-old girl. **Charlotte Haze;** Lolita's mother. **Clare Quilty**, a playwright and friend of Lolita's mother.

SETTING: The novel is set in America from 1947 to 1952.

ADAPTATIONS: In 1962,<u>**Stanley Kubrick**</u> adapted this novel into a film, and in 1997 <u>Adrian Lyne</u>in made a film on it.

SYMBOLS: The Enchanted Hunters,where Humbert first rapes Lolita, is a symbol for pedophiles like Quilty and Humbert. **Nymphet** symbolizes sexually attractive young girl.

Sunglasses symbolize the mystical connection between Annabel and Lolita. **Butterflies,** symbolizes fragile beautiful, often chased and trapped for their beauty. **McFate** represents false fate

QUOTES:

"I see nothing for the treatment of my misery but the ... articulate art."

"The refuge of art.And this is the only immortality you and I may share, my Lolita."

POINTS TO REMEMBER:

- Edgar Alan Poe is his favourite poet and the poem "Annabel Lee" is alluded many times in the novel and Humbert Humbert's first love, Annabel Leigh, is named after the "maiden" in the poem.
- John Ray, the Psychologist, wrote the foreword, and Vladimir Nabokov wrote the afterword to the novel.

46. The Trial (1925)

AUTHOR: Franz Kafka

GENRE: Allegory

TITLE: The title, *The Trial*, refers to the legal case brought against the protagonist Josef K

THEME: Justice and the Law, Absurd, Ambiguity: Guilt and Innocence

PLOT: It tells the story of Josef K, a man arrested and prosecuted by a remote, inaccessible authority, with the nature of his crime revealed neither to him nor to the reader.

MAJOR CHARACTERS: Josef K is a rather arrogant, haughty, and ambitious man. **Dr. Huld,** the lawyer, is an opaque and mysterious character. **Leni** is an attractive young nurse, Dr. Huld, who is seductive and flirtatious.

SETTING: The action of the story begins at K's lodging house, then shifts to the court offices, which are located in an impoverished neighborhood. The rest of the action takes place at K's bank, his lawyer Huld's apartment, a cathedral, and finally, a stone quarry outside the town where K is executed.

ADAPTATIONS: In 1993, Harold Pinter penned the screenplay for the film adaption of *The Trial*.

SYMBOLS: The Court: Tenement and Attic symbolizes the lowly status of the accused and lower-level court officials. **Oppressive Air**, fowl air represents the oppression of the accused by the court system.

QUOTES:

"Having a trial like that means losing a trial like that."

"You don't need to accept everything as true, you only have to accept it as necessary."

REVIEWS/CRITICISM:

- Literary critics have viewed *The Trial* as an allegory for inhuman bureaucracy.

POINTS TO REMEMBER:

- *The Trial* explores the absurdity of life controlled by remote, incomprehensible, and irrational authority.

- Kafka's deep resentment and anger at his father is woven into many of his writings, especially in the cruel and arbitrary authority of the law as described in *The Trial*.

- The book shows a heavy influence of <u>Dostoyevsky</u>'s *<u>Crime and Punishment</u>* and *<u>The Brothers Karamazov</u>*.

47. *The Metamorphosis (1915)*

AUTHOR: Franz Kafka

GENRE: Short Story, Novella, Fantasy Fiction, Psychological Fiction, Absurdist Fiction

TITLE: The title of Kafka's novella, *The Metamorphosis*, refers to the metamorphosis, or change, the protagonist Gregor Samsa, a salesman experiences as he transforms from a human into an insect-like creature.

THEME: Alienation in Modern Life, Mind and Body, Family Ties

PLOT: *Metamorphosis* is the story of a family in which GregorSamsa- the protagonist, suffers a terrible and inexplicable misfortune of transforming into monstrous vermin, and is reduced to an abject and alien state, then is made to suffer doubly by the attitude of his ostensible loved ones. He craves for love and affection, which has been deprived in spite of appealing for love from his family. He receives compassion only from his sister, Grete, with whom the real metamorphosis happens as woman, daughter, and sister. At last, the family makes it clear that they would be better off without him – a verdict that he, with a passivity that seems culpable, accepts.

MAJOR CHARACTERS: GregorSamsa, the protagonist who found himself transformed all of a sudden into a venomous insect; **Grete Samsa**, Gregor's 17-year-old sister, who treats him with compassion. Mr. & Mrs. Samsa - the parents

SETTING: The novella happens in the small apartment of Mr. Gregor

SYMBOLS: Vermin represents dehumanizing and degrading aspects of his life and work in the modern world. **Woman in Furs,** symbolizes Kafka's last hope on humanity. **Mr. Samsa's Uniform** symbolizes self-respect. **Spring** symbolizes hope and new life for the family. **Apples** symbolize the new understanding that leads the world to mystery. **Grete** symbolizes indeterminacy and self-liberation.

QUOTES:

"It'll be the death of both of you, I can see it coming."

"Oh, God ... What a strenuous career it is that I've chosen!"

REVIEWS/CRITICISM:

Vladimir Nabokov, the Russian and American novelist has commented on Kafka's style, he writes: "The transparency of his style underlines the dark richness of his fantasy world. Contrast and uniformity, style and the depicted, portrayal and fable are seamlessly intertwined."

POINTS TO REMEMBER:

- In 1915, the dramatist Carl Sternheim, winner of the prestigious Theodor Fontane prize, bestowed his prize money on Kafka as a mark of writer-to-writer respect.

48. *The Tin Drum (1959)*

AUTHOR: Günther Grass, Polish writer

GENRE: Magical Realism, Bildungsroman, Satire, War Literature, Fame Story

TITLE: The title, *The Tin Drum*, refers to the gift Oskar receives from his mother when he was three years old, and he stopped speaking but beat drums to communicate.

THEME: Nazism and German Guilt, Manipulation versus Growth, Family, Life and Home, and Language.

PLOT: *The Tin Drum* is the story of Oskar Matzerath, the narrator, who narrates everything while his stay in a mental asylum. On his third birthday, Oskar decides to stop growing. Haunted by the deaths of his parents and wielding his tin drum, he recounts the events of his extraordinary life; from the long nightmare of the Nazi era to his anarchic adventures in post-war Germany.

MAJOR CHARACTERS: Oskar Matzerath, receives a red and white enameled tin drum as a gift; **Agnes Koljaiczek**, Oskar's mother who loves her cousin Jan Bronski but marries Alfred Matzerath; **Jan Bronski**, cousin and lover of Agnes, a Polish postal clerk; **Alfred Matzerath**, turns a blind eye to his wife

Agnes's affair with her cousin Jan; **Maria Truczinski ,** the sales girl in Alfred's shop with whom Oskar has his first sexual experience; **Bruno Münsterbergi**s Oskar's caretaker and an artist; **Anna KoljaiczekBronski,** Oskar's grandmother, an elderly potato seller who is devoted to her daughter, Agnes.

SETTING: Oskar's hometown, the city of Danzig.

ADAPTATIONS: In 1979, the novel was adapted into a movie produced by Volker Schlöndorff, caused a controversy in the United States, on the same year it won both the Palme d'Or, and the Academy Award for Best Foreign Language Film the following year.

SYMBOLS: Oskar's Tin Drum symbolizes his outcry against the middle-class mentality of his family and neighborhood, **The Four Skirts** symbolize sexual experiences as well as an escape from responsibility, **Broken glass** symbolizes rage, uniform. **Nurses** symbolize safety and comfort for Oskar, **The Black Cook**, a witchlike figure, is symbolic of death.

QUOTES:

"Is there any other shape in the world so admirably suited to the human form?"

"I began to drum, told it all in order, in the beginning was the beginning."

"I educated myself and formed my own judgments."

"Title: Mystical, barbaric, bored."

POINTS TO REMEMBER:

- *The Tin Drum* earned Grass the title of Germany's "moral conscience" because he freely and forcefully acknowledged the ugliness of Germany's actions.

- Gunter Grass was awarded the Nobel Prize in the year 1999.

- Grass gained a reputation as the "conscience of his generation."

- *The Tin Drum* Widely acclaimed, it was the first in a trilogy of novels referred to as the "Danzig trilogy." The second work in the trilogy, *Cat and Mouse*, published in 1961, is a novella about a parentless, physically deformed only child. Published in 1963, the third novel, *Dog Years* (chronicles the friendship between an Aryan youth and a half-Jewish boy in the WWII).

- The Nobel Committee called this fiction as "black fable."

- Grass said that the epitaph on his gravestone should read "I kept silent."

- A translation into English by Ralph Manheim was published in 1961. A new 50th anniversary translation into English by Breon Mitchell was published in 2009.

49.The Good Earth (1931)

AUTHOR: Pearl S. Buck

GENRE: Historic fiction

TITLE: The title, *The Good Earth,* refers to Wang Lung, the protagonist's attachment to land and its importance.

THEME: Rich vs. Poor, the Oppression of Women, Family, Connection to the Earth, Social Status

PLOT: The plot is a powerful story of a sincere farmer, Wang Lung, and his dedicated wife, O Lan's life in the agrarian China. The story begins with their wedding. The couple nurture their land and family but hard times force them to leave their land and go to the city for survival. His mercy towards a nobleman during the working people riot in China helps his to regain his land and become prosperous in his place. Yet Wang Lung faces a setback in his life due to change of character when he becomes rich.

MAJOR CHARACTERS: Wang Lung, is the main character, **O-lan**, is Wang Lung's wife. She's a quiet, hardworking woman; **NungEn**, the first son who finished his education and lives a luxurious life; **NungWen,** The second son, a prudent and responsible business man; **Pool Fool**, the mentally affected daughter.

SETTING: Set in the south of China.

ADAPTATIONS: In1937,*The Good Earth*, which was based on the stage version of the book, was more successful.

SYMBOLS: The House of Hwang represents the wealth and what the protagonist aspires in life, **The Land** represents Wang Lung's attachment to it, **Opium** represents the destruction of the wealthy people, **The Pearls** symbolise O-lan's appreciation for beauty.

POINTS TO REMEMBER:

- It is the first book in a trilogy with *Sons* (1932) and *A House Divided* (1935).

- The book has won the Pulitzer Prize for Fiction in 1932, and was influential in Buck's winning the Nobel Prize for Literature in 1938.

- Buck, who grew up in China as the daughter of missionaries, wrote the book while living in China and drew on her first-hand observation of Chinese village life.

50. The Guide (1956)

AUTHOR: R.K.Narayan

GENRE: Fiction

TITLE: The title of the novel, *The Guide*, refers to Raju, a tourist guides as well as a passionate lover.

THEME: Hypocrisy and Disguise, a Transformation and Redemption, Gender and Feminism, Tradition versus Modernity, and Greed and Materialism.

PLOT: The novel tracks the development and transformation of the protagonist, Raju, from being a tour guide to a spiritual guide and then one of the greatest holy men of India.

MAJOR CHARACTERS: Raju, the protagonist; **Rosie / Nalini,** the young and beautiful wife of Marco, and love object of Raju; **Marco Polo,** the husband of Rosie, reticent scholar of ancient civilizations.

SETTING: The fictional town of Malgudi in South India.

ADAPTATIONS: In 1968, the novel was adapted into a play, and the play was profiled in the **William Goldman** book *The Season: A Candid Look at Broadway.*

SYMBOLS: The Railway represents modernism and industrialization, **The Serpent** symbolises feminine power, **Nataraja,** a spiritual symbol for dancing, **Water** stands for purification, **Malgudi** represents the country, India, as a whole.

QUOTES:

"It seems to me that we generally do not have a correct measure of our own wisdom."

"The unbeaten brat will remain unlearned."

POINTS TO REMEMBER:

- R. K. Narayan is the pen name suggested by his patron Graham Greene, the 20 century English Novelist, instead of his full name, Rasipuram KrishnaswamiIyerNarayanaswami to R. K. Narayan, so as to be more palatable to English-speaking people.
- R. K. Narayan is the first writer to receive the Sahitya Academy Award.

51. Swami and Friends (1935)

AUTHOR: R.K. Narayan

GENRE: Fiction, Coming-of-Age Novel or Bildungsroman, Socio-cultural Satire

TITLE: Graham Greene, the English novelist, proposed this title, *Swami and Friends*, to its original title Swami, the Tate, suggesting that it would have the advantage of having some resemblance to Rudyard Kipling's *Stalky & Co*.

THEMES: The Political and the Personal under British Colonial Rule,

PLOT: R. K. Narayan captures the pre-independence situation in India. The protagonist Swami, who is a ten-year-old school boy runs away from school, friends and family was drawn heavily to the turmoil that is prevalent in India. Swami is ignorant of the causes of the turmoil he learn what is humanity and the turmoil helps him to understands life in a better way.

MAJOR CHARACTERS: Swaminathan, the ten-year-old protagonist of the novel; **Rajam** is the son of the Police Superintendent; **Mani,** known as "the Mighty Good-For-Nothing;" **"The Pea,"** whose real name is Samuel, is a small boy in Swami's class; **Sankar,** the brilliant boy in the class.

SETTING: The fictional town of Malgudi in South India.

ADAPTATIONS: In 1986, *Swami and Friends* was adapted by actor-director Shankar Nag into the television drama series "Malgudi Days." R. K. Narayan's brother and acclaimed cartoonist R. K. Laxman was the sketch artist.

SYMBOLS: Swami's Cap symbolizes Swami's naiveté about political matters. **Cricket,** symbol of the complex way that English colonization plays out in the lives of Swami and his friends, **The Book of Fairy Tales** symbolizes maturity in the boys.

QUOTES

> "Friendship was another illusion like love, though it did not reach the same mad heights. People pretended that they were friends, when the fact was they were brought together by force of circumstances."

REVIEWS/CRITICISM

The renowned critic C.D. Narasimhaiah remarked: "few writers have been more Indian."

POINTS TO REMEMBER

- R. K. Narayan first published book *Swami and Friends* championed by the English author Graham Greene, his friend and mentor.

- Graham Greene compared R. K. Narayan tragicomedy, pathos, and disappointed aspirations of his characters to that of the Russian Writer Anton Chekhov.

- In *Swami and Friend,* R. K. Narayan created the imaginary microcosmic town- Malgudi.

- This book is first in a trilogy of Malgudi coming-of-age novels, followed by *The Bachelor of Arts* and *The English Teacher*.

- R. K. Narayan is the first among Indian novelists to write exclusively in English about routine life style in India.

- Narayan inscribed in the first page his indebtedness to Graham Greene: "But for you, Swami should be in the bottom of the Thames now".

52. *Kanthapura (1938)*

AUTHOR: Raja Rao

GENRE: Fiction, Sthalapurana

TITLE: The title of the novel is borrowed from the village Kanthapura.

THEMES: Oral Tradition, Writing, Political Power, Gandhi-ism and the Erosion of Caste, Nationalism and Colonialism.

PLOT: The novel records the Gandhian impact on a typical Indian village from the perspective of an old woman of the village, Achakka. It is narrated in the form of a SthalaPurana. It narrates the story of a traditional village in the southern part of India, which is dominated by Brahmins, while lower casts such as Pariahs are marginalized. Despite this classist system, the village retains its long-cherished traditions of festivals in which all castes interact and the villagers are united. The village is believed to be protected by a local deity, Kenchamma.

MAJOR CHARACTERS: Achakka, the narrator from the village of kanthapura; **Moorthy,** the central protagonist, who leaves the village to study in city; and **Rangamma**, a widow in Kanthapura.

SETTING: Kanthapura, a small village in Southwest India 1930.

SYMBOLS: Kenchamma Hill symbolizes the villagers' deep cultural and physical sense of connection to the land, **The River Himavathy** represents the idea of purity, **Kanthapura** symbolizes a living microcosm of India's colonial system.

QUOTES

"There is but one force in life and that is Truth, and there is but one love in life and that is love of mankind, and there is but one God in life and that is the God of all"

"One has to convey in a language that is not one's own the spirit that's one's own".

POINTS TO REMEMBER

- Rao was awarded the Neustadt International Prize for Literature in 1988.
- Raja Rao is one of the pioneers of Indian novel in English.
- He is the recipient of Padma Bhusan and Padma Vibushan, the second and the third highest civilian award in India.
- In Chapter 46 of Kanthapura, Raja Rao has used the connective for 321 times.

53. Nectar in a Sieve (1954)

AUTHOR: Kamala Markandaya

GENRE: Semi-autobiographical Fiction

TITLE: The title *Nectar in a Sieve* is an imagery which implies to enjoy the pleasures of life before it slips away. The title of the novel is taken from the 1825 poem "Work without Hope", by Samuel Taylor Coleridge. An excerpt from the poem is the epigraph of the novel: "Work without hope draws **nectar in a sieve** and hope without an object cannot live."

THEMES: Optimism, Survival, Education, Change, Man versus Nature, Hunger, Starvation.

PLOT: The novel revolves around the narrator Rukmani, who represents a common peasant in India; and how her life changes in independent India. Rukmani, the daughter of the village headman was given as a child bride to a tenant farmer, Nathan. She works along with her husband hopefully to face the huge hindrances in her life in the form of droughts, monsoon, insects etc. Rukmani has to fight continuously till the end, to care for her loved ones.

MAJOR CHARACTERS: Rukmani, the narrator who marries Nathan at the age of 12; **Nathan,** an uneducated rice farmer; **Irawaddy**, the beautiful daughter of Rukmani, who starts her life with a bright future and ends up becoming prostitute;

Kennington, the Western doctor, **Kunthi**, a prostitute acts as the novel's main antagonist.

SETTING: Set in Tamil Nadu of British India around 1930s.

SYMBOLS: The cobra symbolizes deceit. **Rice** is a symbol of fertility and life. **Bullocks** symbolize the hard-working peasants. **Tannery** symbolizes modernity. **Learning** is a symbol of hope. **Drums** symbolize times of great change.

QUOTES

"Bend like the grass,that you do not break."

"Want is our companion from birth to death, familiar as the seasons or the earth." "There is a limit to the achievements of human courage."

"Change I had known before, and it had been gradual. But the change that now came into my life, into all our lives, blasting its way into our village, seemed wrought in the twinkling of an eye."

REVIEWS/CRITICISM

Meenakshi Mukerjee on what she observed in the *Nectar in a Sieve* comments: "Change is seen on a broader scale in the context of a whole village or town, at different levels of artistic success."

POINTS TO REMEMBER

- Markandaya was one of the first to present complex Indian women in fiction.

- *Nectar in a Sieve* is the first novel in India which recalls its savage power and authentic atmosphere of China's "The Good Earth".
- Kamala Puraniya Taylor is Markandaya's original name and she wrote in the name of Kamala Markandaya.
- The novel progresses using the flashback technique and ends where it begins like Arundathi Roy's *God of Small Things*.

54. Train to Pakistan (1956)

AUTHOR: Khushwant Singh

GENRE: Historical Fiction

TITLE: The title signifies the groups or multitudes of people who are migrating to different places in search of shelter.

THEMES: The Partition of India and Religious Warfare, Postcolonial Anxiety and National Identity, Power and Corruption, Honor and Heroism, Gender and Masculinity.

PLOT: *Train to Pakistan* is a poignant story of the troubled days during partition. Khushwant Singh tries to portray the reality of partition in 1947. It primarily deals with India's independence and the subsequent violence on both sides of the border. Hukum Chand, the magistrate of Chundunnuger, feels a sting of helplessness to stop the communal violence; and tries to live in peace facing all kinds of turmoil.

MAJOR CHARACTERS: Juggut Singh is a Sikh peasant who is jailed; **Nooran**isa Muslim girl and the beloved of Juggut; **Iqbal Singh**, communist and politician;**Hukum Chand,** the magistrate and deputy commissioner; **Mahatma Gandhi**, an Indian lawyer, politician, and writer.

SETTING: The novel is set in a small village, Mano Majra,inthe India-Pakistan Border, India.

ADAPTATIONS: In 1998, a movie was released based on this novel with the same title and it was nominated in Cinequest Film Festival.

SYMBOLS: Antimony is a symbol of the pleasures. **The railway bridge** is a symbol of India's connection with Pakistan. **Bangles** represent belief in eternity. **Train to Pakistan** is a symbol of motion or movement.

QUOTES

"Poor people cannot afford to have morals. So they have religion."

"Not forever does the bulbul sing

In balmy shades of bowers,

Not forever lasts the spring

Nor ever blossom the flowers.

Not forever reigneth joy,

Sets the sun on days of bliss,

Friendships not forever last,

They know not life, ho know not this."

POINTS TO REMEMBER

- *Train to Pakistan* offers insight into the lives and customs of Sikhs in India.

- In 1974, Khushwant Singh was awarded the Padma Bhushan as a mark of protest against 'Operation Blue Star,' in which the Indian Army raided Amritsar in 1984.

- In 2007, Singh was awarded the Padma Vibhushan, the second-highest civilian award in India.

- The epitaph of Kushwant Singh bears this inscription: "This is where my roots are. I have nourished them with tears of nostalgia"

55. *The Namesake (2003)*

AUTHOR: JhumpaLahiri

GENRE: Fiction

TITLE: The title, *Namesakei,* refers to the nickname of one main character, Gogol. The nickname stems from Gogol's father Ashoke's love of *The Collected Stories of Nikolai Gogol*, which saved Ashoke's life after a deadly train crash.

THEMES: Importance of Names, Cultural Identity, Starting Over.

PLOT: It is a novel about an immigrant Bengali family's imperfect assimilation with America and at its core, has a poignant father-son relationship and the search for identity when torn between two worlds.

MAJOR CHARACTERS: Gogol Ganguli, the son of Bengali immigrants Ashoke; **Ashoke Ganguli** is a Bengali immigrant who flees to the United States from Calcutta; **Ashima Ganguli,** Gogol's mother; **Sonali,** the younger of the two Ganguli children.

SETTING: The novel is set in Boston, U.S.A; and Calcutta, India.

ADAPTATIONS: In 2006, Mira Nairdirected the movie adaption of the novel which was released in the United States, Canada, United Kingdom, and India.

SYMBOLS: The Overcoatis a symbol of Gokul father's love and deep ties to his family. **Gangulis' House on Pemberton road** symbolizes strong connection to culture. **Gogol's name, Nikhil,**

symbolizes the need to keep the Bengali naming tradition. **Train** symbolizes journey of life through bad and good things. **Relationships** symbolize the characters' search for true identity.

QUOTES

"Pack a pillow and a blanket and see as much of the world as you can."

"Instead of thanking God he thanks Gogol, the Russian writer who had saved his life."

"We went together to a place where there was nowhere left to go."

POINTS TO REMEMBER

- In 1999, Jhumpa Lahiri was awarded the Pulitzer Prize PEN/Hemingway Award for *Interpreter of Maladies*.

56. The Inheritance of loss (2006)

AUTHOR: Kiran Desai

GENRE: Domestic Fiction

TITLE: The title *The Inheritance of Loss* signifies plainly and literally as it appears in the title.

THEMES: Colonialism and Globalization, Poverty vs. Privilege, Home and Belonging, Gender and Misogyny.

PLOT: The plot beautifully interconnects two truncated families of a retired judge, who lives in an isolated house at the foot of Mount Kanchenjunga in the Himalayas for peace, where his granddaughter Sai arrives. Sai was taken care by the judge's cook, who idealises and worries over his son Biju, who is struggling in New York restaurant as an illegal immigrant.

MAJOR CHARACTERS: Jemubhai, the judge; **Sai,** the judge's granddaughter; **Biju**, the cook's son who travels to New York; **Gyan**, Sai's twenty-year-old Nepali math tutor; **Nimi,** the judge's wife and Sai's maternal grandmother.

SETTING: The novel is set in India and United States Himalayas in Sai's grandfather's house.

SYMBOLS: The Powder Puff symbolises the judge's adoption of British culture and rejection of Indian culture, **Rats** represents the abuse of poor people of the society, **Kukris** symbolise dedication and violence.

REVIEWS/CRITICISM: The New York Times claimed Desai "manages to explore, with intimacy and insight, just about every contemporary international issue: globalization, multiculturalism, economic inequality, fundamentalism and terrorist violence."

POINTS TO REMEMBER

- In 2006, Kiran Desai won the Man Booker Prize of the Year for her second novel *The Inheritance of Loss*
- The Gorkhaland movement is used as a historic backdrop to the novel *The Inheritance of Loss*
- In 1998, Kiran Desai did the Pastiche reworking of **R.K. Narayan's** *The Guide*

57.*The Shadow Lines (1988)*

AUTHOR: Amitav Gosh

GENRE: Historical Fiction, Bildungsroman

TITLE: The title *The Shadow Lines* represents the illusionary lines created by the nations as boundary lines, the lines that are both arbitrary and invented.

THEMES: Youth vs. Maturity, Freedom and Identity, Partition, Violence.

PLOT: The novel *The Shadow Lines* takes the reader to the narrator, who has hero worship towards his uncle Tridib who feeds him with his memories of his visit to London and of the grandmother's nostalgic memories of West Bengal. The story spans three generations of the narrator's family.

MAJOR CHARACTERS: The Narrator, Tridib is the narrator's uncle, who is in love with May; **Ila,** Ila is the narrator's cousin; **Tha'mma,** the narrator's grandmother; **May Price,** May is Mrs. Price's daughter.

SETTING: The settings of the novel are Calcutta, Dhaka, British London, England.

SYMBOLS: The Upside-Down House represents the polarizing power of borders.

QUOTES

"I know nothing of this silence except that it lies outside the reach of my intelligence, beyond words - that is why this silence must win, must inevitably defeat me, because it is not a presence at all."

"People like my grandmother, who have no home but in memory, learn to be very skilled in the art of recollection."

"Nobody knows, nobody can ever know, not even in memory, because there are moments in time that are not knowable."

POINTS TO REMEMBER:

- Amitav Ghosh in his Ibis trilogy (*Sea of Poppies, River of Smoke, and Flood of Fire*) explores the colonial history of the area around the Bay of Bengal, the Arabian Sea, and the Indian Ocean.

- *The shadow lines* is split into two parts "Going Away" and "Coming Home."

- Do you remember? Is the persistent question in the novel which shapes the narrators search for connections.

- In 1998, *The Shadow Lines* won the Sahitya Akademi Award.

- The novel is set against the backdrop of historical events such as Swadeshi movement, Second World War, Partition of India and Communal riots of 1963-64 in Dhaka and Calcutta.

58. The Hungry Tide (2004)

AUTHOR: Amitav Gosh

GENRE: Environmental Fiction

TITLE: The novel's title *The Hungry tide* represents the adverse power of nature. In this novel the title metaphorically, refers to the emotional tide of the characters.

THEMES: Language, Man vs Nature, Environmental Conservation, Idealism vs Practicality.

PLOT: Piya, an American of Bengali origin and a cetologist, comes to Sudarbans in search of dolphins. She meets Kanai, a sophisticated Delhi Businessman comes to visit his widowed aunt becomes her translator in her conversation with Fokir, the fisherman, who assisted Priya to look for dolphins and the proximity brings them close to the real tide happens in the minds of the character.

MAJOR CHARACTERS: Piya Roy , Piya is a cetologist; **Kanai Dut**t, a wealthy middle-aged businessman translator in new Delhi; **Nirmal Bose,** Nilima's husband; **Nilima**, who is known simply as Mashima; **kanai's Aunt**; **Fokir**, the proud and poor fisherman,

SETTING: The novel is set in The Sundarbans, a maze of floating islands covered with mangroves which is prone to danger in 1950s.

SYMBOLS: The cyclone shelter symbolizes Nirmal's willingness to compromise belief for unadulterated communist theory, **Tigerss** symbolise the extraordinary power of nature, **Gamchhas** symbolise one's connection to places people and culture.

QUOTES:

"beauty is nothing but the start of terror we can hardly bear, and we adore it because of the serene scorn it could kill us with . . ."

> "It would be enough; as an alibi for a life, it would do; she would not need to apologize for how she had spent her time on this earth."

POINTS TO REMEMBER

- The novel is divided into two parts- "The Ebb -:Bhata" and "The Flood- Jowar."
- In 2004, *The Hungry Tide* has won the Hutch Crossword Book Award for Fiction.

59. *The White Tiger (2008)*

AUTHOR: Aravind Adiga

GENRE: Picaresque novel, Mystery, Epistolary novel

TITLE: The title is significant for both Balram and the tiger, who are unique. Balram earns this nickname when he impresses a visiting school official with his intelligence and reading skills. *The White Tiger* is a symbol for rare talent and only one in 10000 Bengali tigers are white.

THEMES: The Self-Made Man, Social Breakdown, Self-Interest, Corruption, Education, Family, Morality and Indian Society.

PLOT: *The White Tiger* portrays the life of Balram Halwai, a village boy and a son of a puller who journey's to Delhi and murders his employer and eventually rises as a successful businessman.

MAJOR CHARACTERS: Balram Halwai, "Munna" boy, the protagonist and narrator; **Mr. Ashok**, Balram's employer; **Kusum**, the matriarch of Balram's family, his grandmother; **Pinky** ,Ashok's beautiful, Americanized wife.

SETTING: *The White Tiger* takes place in modern day India.

SYMBOLS: The White Tiger symbolises the empowerment of Balram and the rare talent, **The Rooster Coop** represents of oppression of poor, **The Black Fort** symbolises extreme poverty, darkness and fear , **Chandelier** symbolises light, **Delhi City** Symbolises rich and poor life.

QUOTES

"They remain slaves because they can't see what is beautiful in this world."

"Stories of rottenness and corruption are always the best stories, aren't they?"

"I absorbed everything—that's the amazing thing about entrepreneurs. We are like sponges—we absorb and grow."

POINTS TO REMEMBER:

- *The White Tiger* is the debut novel of Aravind Adiga
- Aravind Adiga is the second youngest writer to receive the Man Booker prize
- American novelists—Richard Wright, James Baldwin, and Ralph Ellison—as his primary influences in writing *The White Tiger.*
- In 2008, *The White Tiger* won the Man-Booker

60. The God of Small Things (1997)

AUTHOR: Arundhati Roy

GENRE: Fiction

TITLE: The title *The God of Small Things* directly refers to the main themes that the day-to-day life's "small things" affects "big things" such as politics, racism, and culture.

THEMES: Obligations, Class Division, Small Things, Love.

PLOT: The novel *The God of Small Things* takes place in a small village called Ayemenem in Kerala, the characters in the novel are tossed from Ayemenem to England, then to America, Shillong, and Delhi and back to Ayemenem, badly battered, badly bruised. It portrays the painful childhood of Rahel and Estha, fraternal twins and it also portrays a profane love between an untouchable and a respectable lady. The novel is all about how these small things affect the characters behavior and lives.

MAJOR CHARACTERS: Rahel, as a child, Rahel has an incredibly intimate connection with her twin brother **Estha; Ammu; Velutha**, born as a Paravan(an Untouchable) talented untouchable; **Baby Kochamma**, the daughter of a Syrian Christian pries; **Sophie Mol**, Margaret Kochamma's daughter.

SETTING: The setting for *The God of Small Things* is the small village of Ayemenem, in the Kottayam district of the Indian state of Kerala, on the west coast of India.

ADAPTATIONS: In 2013, *Talkhiyaan,* a Pakistani television series based on the novel, was aired on Express Entertainment.

SYMBOLS: **Pappachi's Moth** represents his anger and fear, **Paradise Pickles & Preserves**, **Rahel's Watch**, it symbolize how events of that night will freeze Rahel and Estha there for the rest of their lives, **Plymouth** represents the importance of manhood.

QUOTES

"It was a time when the unthinkable becomes thinkable and the impossible really happened."

"If he held her, he couldn't kiss her. If he kissed her, he couldn't see her. If he saw her, he couldn't feel her"

POINTS TO REMEMBER

- In 1997, *The God of Small Things* won the Man- Booker prize.

- "Fiction is truth. I think fiction is the truest thing there ever was." - Arundhati Roy

61. *Murder in the Cathedral (1935)*

AUTHOR: T.S.Eliot

GENRE: Drama, Verse Drama, Christian Tragedy

TITLE: The title refers to the murder of the Archbishop Thomas Becket of Canterbury in the Cathedral of the city.

THEMES: Worldly Power vs. Spiritual Power, Fate and Sacrifice, Temptation, Eternity and Human Understanding, Loyalty and Guilt.

PLOT: *Murder in the Cathedral* portrays the assassination of Archbishop Thomas Becket in Canterbury Cathedral during the reign of Henry II in 1170.

MAJOR CHARACTERS: Thomas Becket, the Archbishop of Canterbury; **The Chorus** made up of common women of Canterbury; **The Priests, Four Tempter**, former friend of both Becket and the king; **four knights, King Henry II.**

SETTING: The drama was set in Canterbury, England, in December of 1170, when Archbishop Thomas Becket of Canterbury returned from France.

ADAPTATIONS: In 1951, Austrian director George Hoellering directed the movie in black and white and won the Grand Prix at the Venice Film Festival.

SYMBOLS: Martyrdom, the emblem of Becket's radical submission to God. **The Wheel** represents the wholeness and indivisibility of divine.

QUOTES

"Unreal friendship may turn to real

But real friendship, once ended, cannot be mended"

"The last temptation is the greatest treason: To do the right

deed for the wrong reason."

"A christian martyrdom is never an accident, for Saints are

not made by accident."

"It is the just man who like a bold lion, should be without

fear."

"It is out of time that my decision is taken

If you call that decision

To which my whole being gives entire consent.

I give my life

To the Law of God above the Law of Man."

POINTS TO REMEMBER

- Eliot drew his play *Murder in the Cathedral* heavily on the writing of <u>Edward Grim</u>, a clerk who was an eyewitness to the event.

- T. S Eliot was a pioneer of Modernist Movement in Literature

- He was awarded the Nobel Prize for Literature in 1948.

- The four knights who murdered Bishop are Reginald Fitz, Hugh De Morville, Willaim de Tracy, Richard le Breton

- The play action starts from 2 December and ends in 29 December 1170.

- The bishop encounters Four temptations and the fourth temptation is martyrdom.

62. *Waiting for Godot (1953)*

AUTHOR: Samuel Beckett, Irish playwright

GENRE: Tragic comedy

TITLE: The title refers to the waiting of the two central characters Vladmir and Estragon for someone called Godot, who never arrives. The title also emphasis on the futility of human existence.

THEMES: Absurdity of Existence, Purposelessness of Life, Uncertainty of Life, Folly of Seeking Meaning.

PLOT: The play revolves around the conversation between the two characters Estragon and Vladimir while waiting for the arrival of a person called Godot, who never appears but keeps on sending word repeatedly about his arrival. In this process of waiting, they encounter Pozzo and Lucky which reminds them of the miseries of life. Their only hope for enlightenment is the arrival of Godot and their waiting makes them noble.

MAJOR CHARACTERS: Estragon and Vladimir, the two primary characters; **Pozzo**, Wealthy landowner; **Lucky**, Pozzo's slave.

SETTING: Country Road with a single tree present.

ADAPTATIONS: A web series adaptation titled *While Waiting for Godot* was also directed by Rudi Azank and produced at New

York University in 2013, setting the story among the modern-day New York homeless.

SYMBOLS: Leafless tree represents the organic element that is dead and dormant, **Lucky's Baggage, Pozzo's rope** represents balance of power.

QUOTES

"The tears of the world are a constant quantity. For each one who begins to weep somewhere else another stops. The same is true of the laugh."

"Nothing happens. Nobody comes, nobody goes. It's awful."

"To every man his little cross. Till he dies. And is forgotten."

POINTS TO REMEMBER

- **Theatre of Absurd** are plays in which lack of purpose and logic creates uncertainty, hopelessness, and humour

- subtitled (in English only) "a tragicomedy in two acts"

- He is the recipient of noble prize in 1969

- His play *Come and Go* is a stark dramaticule with three female characters and a text of 121 words

- *Breath* is a 30 second play by Beckett

- He Wrote three plays *Waiting for Godot, Endgame* and *Happy Days* deals with human struggle and survival

63. The Birthday Party (1958)

AUTHOR: Harold Pinter

GENRE: Drama, "Comedy of Menace," Theatre of the Absurd

TITLE: The title *The Birthday Party* refers to the birthday party of Stanley who insists it is not his birthday.

THEMES: Ambiguity, Meaninglessness, Absurdity, Guilt and Transgression, Order, Chaos, Sanity, Isolation, Freedom, Independence.

PLOT: In *The Birthday Party* Stanley Webber, an out of work pianist, who lives in a rundown boarding house run by Meg and Petey Boles, in an English seaside town, is mysteriously threatened and taken over by two sinister strangers, Goldberg and McCann, arrive looking for him, supposedly on his birthday, and in turn his apparently-innocuous birthday party organized by Meg turns into a nightmare.

MAJOR CHARACTERS: Stanley Webber, the pianist in Meg and Petey Boles's boarding house; **Meg Boles and Petey,** owners of the boarding house; **Goldberg and McCann,** the two strangers in search of Stanley; **Lulu,** a young woman who visits Meg and Petey's boarding house.

SETTING: A rundown boarding house in a coastal English resort town.

ADAPTATIONS: In 1968, the drama was adapted into a movie *The Birthday Party* directed by William Friedkin. The screenplay for the film was written by Pinter himself.

SYMBOLS: Stanley's Drum represents meg's fondness for order**, WheelBarrow** symbolises the hearse and coffin, **Mirror** symbolises the self reflection of the characters, **window** symbolises the hope of escape and its meaninglessness.

QUOTES:

"I know the place.

It is true.

Everything we do

Corrects the space

Between death and me

And you."

"I can't really articulate what I feel,"

"Good writing excites me, and makes life worth living."

POINTS TO REMEMBER

- Pinter is associated with the Theatre of the Absurd.
- He won the Nobel Prize in Literature in 2005
- *The Birthday Party* is similar to Kafka's unfinished novel, *The Trial*, which examines the ways in which its protagonist, Joseph K.,
- In his acceptance speech of Nobel prize he attacked the US invasion on Iraq
- He is the inventor of new type of comedy called 'Comedy of Menance', it means a play set in an enclosed place and the characters express doubt and fear.

64. Rosencrantz and Guildenstern are Dead (1966)

AUTHOR: Tom Stoppard, Jewish British novelist

GENRE: Absurdist, Existential Tragicomedy

TITLE: The title of the play is taken from Shakespeare's play *Hamlet* where the ambassador laments that everyone is dead.

THEMES: Uncertainty, Religion vs Science, Free Will vs Destiny, Death.

PLOT: The play portrays the same plot of Shakespeare's Hamlet from the perspective of the two minor characters Rosencrantz and Guildenstern, whereas the major characters of Shakespeare's Hamlet becomes the minor characters including Hamlet and the play is dominated by the conversation between the two characters, raising questions, interrupting each other and remaining silent. Whatever happens off stage in Hamlet becomes on stage and the play ends with the same scene of Hamlet where the ambassador comes and tells that Rosencrantz and Guildenstern are dead.

MAJOR CHARACTERS: Rosencratz and Guildenstern, childhood friends of Hamlet; **Gertude,** Hamlet's mother; **Hamlet,** Prince of Denmark; **Claudius**, king of Denmark and Hamlet's step father.

SETTING: An undisclosed location in the wilderness, Elsinore, England.

ADAPTATIONS: In 1990, *Rosencrantz and Guildenstern are Dead* was turned into a movie, with screenplay and direction by Stoppard.

SYMBOLS: Coin symbolises tension of opposites, **Boat** symbolises final destination.

QUOTES

> "Look on every exit as being an entrance somewhere else."

> "We're actors — we're the opposite of people!"

> "Words, words. They're all we have to go on."

POINTS TO REMEMBER

- The play is compared to Samuel Beckett's *Waiting for Godot* for portraying two central characters as halves of one

- In 1998, Tom Stopard was honoured in Academy Award for the best original screenplay for his play *Shakespeare in Love*

- He was endowed with knighthood for his contribution to theatre in 1997

65. *The Winslow Boy (1964)*

AUTHOR: Terence Mervyn Rattigan

GENRE: Drama

TITLE: The title of the play *The Winslow Boy* refers to Ronnie Winslow.

THEMES: Principles and Sacrifice, family, women and patriarchy, media and spectacle

PLOT: Terrence Rattigan's *The Winslow Boy* is the story of a family that sacrifices everything in order to uphold the "truth." Ronnie Winslow, the boy of the title, is expelled from his Navy College for allegedly stealing a postal order worth just five shillings.

MAJOR CHARACTERS: Ronnie Winslow, the Winslow Boy of the play; **Arthur Winslow**, the intimidating patriarch of the Patriarchal family; **Grace Winslow,** mother of the Winslow boy; **Catherine Winslow**, daughter of Arthur and Grace; **Dickie Winslow** Ronnie's older brother; **Sir Robert Morton**, the barrister; **Violet**, the housemaid.

SETTING: A house in Kensington, London, before WW1.

ADAPTATIONS: *The Winslow Boy* was presented on the BBC Home Service Saturday Night Theatre November 15, 1947. The performance starred David Spenser, Frank Cellier, and Molly Rankin.

SYMBOLS: Gramophone represents the inevitability of societal change as new generations come of age.

QUOTES

> "But the world is a dark enough play **John Watherstone**ce for even a little flicker to be welcome."

> "To love with one's eyes open sometimes makes life very difficult."

> "To see yourself as the world sees you may be very brave, but it can also be very foolish."

POINTS TO REMEMBER

- *The Winslow Boy* is based on a real-life event about the court case of George Archer-Shee, a naval cadet expelled for stealing a postal order

- A key divergence between the play and the real case, however, is the character of Catherine, who is very conservative in the real case whereas Winslow's sister is quite radical.

- *The Winslow Boy* is one example of the "drawing-room play," in which all the action takes place in a singular location that allows for visitors to come and go.

66. *Top Girls (1980)*

AUTHOR: Caryl Churchill   **GENRE:** Drama

TITLE: The title *Top Girls* refers to Marlene, who is recently promoted to the top Girls employment agency.

THEMES: Life Under the Patriarchy, Women's Stories, Power, Success, Individualism, motherhood

PLOT: Top Girls, the play by Caryl Churchill centres around Marlene, a career-driven woman who is heavily invested in women's success in business. The play examines the roles available to women in modern society, and what it means or takes for a woman to succeed. It also dwells heavily on the cost of ambition and the influence of Thatcherite politics on feminism.

MAJOR CHARACTERS: *Marlene,* the protagonist of the play, is a high ranking official at the Top Girls Employment Agency in London; **Isabella Bird**, is a real-life, nineteenth-century writer and a novelist; **Lady Nijo,**is a real-life concubine-turned into Buddhist-nun; **Dull Gret**, Flemish renaissance painter; **Angie**, is Joyce's sixteen-year-old adoptive daughter.

SETTING: Set in early Thatcherite London, England.

 SYMBOLS: Top girls employment agency is a symbol of corruption and blind individualism of Thatcherism.

QUOTES

"And I hit him with a stick. Yes, I hit him with a stick."

"I put on this dress to kill my mother."

"Christ, what a waste of time."

REVIEWS/CRITICISM

- The famous theatre critic of *Guardian* Michael Billington remarks, *Top Girls* is 'a work of art rather than a social tract; and it acquired a real emotional momentum in the final act' (*State of the Nation*, 2007).
- Caryl Churchill criticises the extreme individualism and hyper professionalism

POINTS TO REMEMBER

- The play stikes a contrast between American feminism, which celebrates individualistic women who acquire power and wealth, and British socialist feminism, which involves collective group gain. It is also comments on **Margaret Thatcher**, the then prime minister, who celebrated personal achievement and believed in free-market capitalism (Thatcherism)
- *Top Girls* is the first play to engage directly on Thatcherism
- The play opens with a dinner party hosted by Marlyne to a host of women from history. The guests include Pope Joan, who famously disguised herself as a man, the explorer Isabella Bird, Dull Gret, Lady Nijo (the Japanese courtesan) and Patient Griselda, the wife from Chaucer's The Clerk's Tale
- *Top Girls* is a feminist play, which parades Thatcherism and feminism to be antithetical.
- The play opens with a dream sequence

67. A Street Car Named Desire (1947)

AUTHOR: Tennssee Williams

GENRE: Drama

TITLE: *A Street Car Named Desire* details the themes of the cycles of violence that is woven through the play.

THEMES: Fantasy/Illusion, The Primitive and the Primal, cruelty, loneliness.

PLOT: *A Streetcar Named Desire* is a play written by Tennessee Williams that opened on Broadway on December 3, 1947. The play is a play of sexual violence repression and it dramatises the moral and mental disintegration of Blanche DuBois, a southern belle who, after encountering a series of personal losses, leaves her aristocratic background seeking refuge with her sister and brother-in-law in a dilapidated New Orleans tenement.

MAJOR CHARACTERS: Blanche DuBois, a girl in thirties lost all her money and ancestral properties; **Stanley Kowalski**, the brother-in -law of Blanche; **Stella Kowalski**, the sister; **Mitch**, the Stanley Kowalski's good friend owner of Belle Reve plantations.

SETTING: The play is set in the French Quarter of New Orleans.

ADAPTATIONS: In 1951, a film adaptation of the play, directed by Elia Kazan, with Malden, Brando, and Hunter reprising their Broadway roles, joined by Vivien Leigh from the London production for the part of Blanche.

SYMBOLS: Shadows and Cries dramatize Blanche's final breakdown and departure from reality in the face of Stanley's physical threat.

QUOTES

> "What is straight? A line can be straight, or a street, but the human heart, oh, no, it's curved like a road through mountains."

> "I have always depended on the kindness of strangers."

> "Show me a person who hasn't known any sorrow and I'll show you a superficial."

> "Oh, you can't describe someone you're in love with!"

POINTS TO REMEMBER

- The production of *A Street Car Named Desire* was strongly influenced by the technique called method developed by the Russian actor and producer Konstantain Stainslavsky

- The play in three acts by Tennessee Williams, first produced and published in 1947 and won the Pulitzer Prize for drama.

- Tennessee Williams in his essay *A Streetcar Named Success* discusses about art and the artist's role in society. ***The Catastrophe of success*** is an essay written as an introduction to *The Glass Menagerie*

68. *The Glass Menagerie (1944)*

AUTHOR: Tennesse Williams

GENRE: Drama

TITLE: The title *The Glass Menagerie* describes Laura Wingfield's collection of tiny glass animals as fragile as Laura herself.

THEMES: Abandonment, disillusionment, Living in the past,

PLOT: *The Glass Menagerie* is a play based on the memory of Tom Wingfield is a tragic family tale where the frustrated mother, persuades her son Tom, who work in a shoe factory hates his job and escapes to movies at night to bring a gentleman caller to her daughter Laura. Laura who is fragile, shy and lame in one leg suffers from inferiority complex and seldom goes out. Tom brings her schoolmate Jim as a gentleman caller for Laura excites her and leaves her devasted and her Unicorn Glass menagerie breaks.

MAJOR CHARACTERS: Tom, the bread winner of the family works in a shoe factory, aspires to become a poet; **Amanda,** middle aged woman who had a good childhood; **Laura,** a young woman who is as fragile as her glass animals; **Jim,** an athlete friend of Tom who encourages Laura.

SETTING: Wingfield family's apartment in St. Louis, Missouri 1937.

ADAPTATIONS:

- There is an Indian adaptation of the play, filmed in the Malayalam language. The movie titled Akale (meaning At a Distance), released in 2004, is directed by Shyamaprasad. The story is set in the southern Indian state of Kerala in the 1970s, in an Anglo-Indian/Latin Catholic household. The characters were renamed to fit the context better (the surname Wingfield was changed to D'Costa, reflecting the part-Portuguese heritage of the family — probably on the absent father's side, since the mother is Anglo-Indian), but the story remains essentially the same.

- Two Hollywood movie versions of *The Glass Menagerie* have been produced. The first, directed by Irving Rapper in 1950, the climax has been changed for the American audience. It was considered the worst adaptation.

SYMBOLS: Glass animals represent the multifaceted Laura and her fragility, **Unicorn** represents Laura's deformity in leg and her uniqueness, **Blue Roses** symbolise her crush towards Jim 'O Corner ,**Fire Escape** represents exit and entry of wingfield family from illusionary world.

QUOTES

"Time is the longest distance between two places."

"Being disappointed is one thing and being discouraged is something else. I am disappointed but I am not discouraged."

"People go to the movies instead of moving."

POINTS TO REMEMBER

- Tennessee Williams based *The Glass Menagerie* on *Portrait of a Girl in Glass.*

- The play has strong autobiographical elements which features his histrionic mother, and mentally fragile sister Laura.

- Williams drew on an earlier short story, as well as a screenplay he had written under the title of *The Gentleman Caller.*

- *The Glass Menagerie* is the first memory play, followed by Harold Pinter's *Old Times and Brian Friel's Dancing at Lughnasa.*

69. *All My Sons (1947)*

AUTHOR: Arthur Miller

GENRE: Drama

TITLE: Joe Keller claims the meaning of solidarity claimed to have shipped faulty aircraft to keep his business alive for his sons who in turn killed 21 pilots because of his crime were also "his sons".

THEMES: Fathers as heads, Personal vs Social responsibility, Idealism vs Practicality.

PLOT: Joe Keller and Herbert Deever, partners in a machine shop during the war, turned out defective airplane parts, causing the deaths of many men. Deever was sent to prison while Keller escaped punishment and went on to make lots of money. In a work of tremendous power, a love affair between Keller's son, Chris, and Ann Deever, Herbert's daughter, to the bitterness of George Keller, who returns from the war to find his father in prison and his father's partner free, and the reaction of a son to his father's guilt escalate towards the climax where Chris shows the letter their parents that reveals that Larry commit suicide feeling sorry for his father's guilt and inturn Joe too commit suicide after hearing this.

MAJOR CHARACTERS: Joe Keller, 60, who has charged with knowingly shipping defective aircraft engine cylinder which kills 21 pilots; **Kate Keller,** the mother who is believes her son Larry will return and always positive; **Chris Keller,** the brother; **Ann**

Deever, young strong woman who loves chris Keller; **George Deever**, brother of Ann; Dr. Jim Bayliss the neighbor.

SETTING: The setting of *All My Sons* is the Keller's backyard in a small Midwestern town shortly after World War II.

ADAPTATIONS: In 1948, *All My Sons* was first adapted into a filand. Edward G. Robinson played Joe Keller. It was directed by Irving Reis and gained two award nominations, Best Written American Drama and The Robert Meltzer Award for the film's co-writer Chester Erskine.

SYMBOLS: Fallen Tree is a symbolic reference to the Biblical Garden of Eden, **Damaged airplane parts** is a symbolic reference to the damaged "heads" as family heads, **Steve Deever hat** represents the injustice done to him by Joe.

QUOTES:

"I know you're no worse than most men but I thought you were better. I never saw you as a man. I saw you as my father."

"You don't realize how people can hate, they can hate so much they'll tear the world to pieces."

"There are certain people, the sicker they get the longer they live."

POINTS TO REMEMBER

- *All My Sons* was the inspiration for the name of the popular band Twenty-One Pilots.
- The working title of the play is *The Sign of the Archer*
- *All My Sons* is a social drama which dramatises ties between the individual and society.
- Norweign Playwright Henrik Ibsen is called the *father of Theatrical Realism.* He is the Progenitor for Athur miller
- The notion of Henrik Ibsen is always traced in *All My Sons.* It is called as **Ibsenesque play**
- All My Sons is based upon a true story of Wright Aeronautical Corporation based in Ohio's conspiracy with army inspection officers to approve defective aircraft engines destined for military use.

70. Death of a Salesman (1949)

AUTHOR: Arthur Miller

GENRE: Drama

TITLE: *Death of a Salesman* refers to the literal and metaphorical death of the salesman Willy Loman. The title comes from the play where a character says "death of a salesman in his green velvet slippers" on his way for another sale.

THEMES: American Dream vs Disillusionment, Illusion vs Reality, Betrayal, Nature vs Man-Made Environment.

PLOT: *Death of a Salesman* dramatises the salesman Willie Loman's attempt to justify himself at the verge of his death and endures the disaster after accepting the false values of the contemporary American society.

MAJOR CHARACTERS: **Willy Loman**, a 60 year old salesman; **Linda Loman** Willy's wife, advocate and defender; **Biff Loman,** 34 year old son of Willy; **Happy Loman** second son of Willy.

SETTING: The play is set in late 1940s at Willy Loman's house in New York City and Barnaby River; Boston set in 1940 in Brooklyn, Manhattan and Boston.

ADAPTATIONS: The play premiered on Broadway in February 1949, running for 742 performances, and has been revived on Broadway four times.

SYMBOLS: Distant Land represents freedom from restraint, **Stockings** symbolise Willy deception and betrayal, **seeds** represent Willy's longing for future, **Flute** symbolises the past for Willy.

QUOTES

"The jungle is dark but full of diamonds, Willy."

"A small man can be just as exhausted as a great man."

"You can't eat the orange and throw the peel away - a man is not a piece of fruit."

"A man is not a bird, to come and go with the springtime."

POINTS TO REMEMBER

- *Death Of a Salesman* is a play in two acts which covers 24 hours period and a Requiem
- It won the 1949 Pulitzer Prize for Drama and Tony Award for Best Play.

71. *The Emperor Jones (1920)*

AUTHOR: Eugene o' Neil

GENRE: tragedy, expressionistic play

TITLE: The title *The Emperor Jones* refers to the emperor king Brutus Jones.

THEMES: Racism, History and Collective Memory, Godliness, Humanity and Fear, Power and Systemic Oppression.

PLOT: Eugene O'Neill's *The Emperor Jones* is a tragedy which presents the rise and fall of Brutus Jones, a resourceful, self-assured African American as an Emperor. Brutus Jones is a former Pullman porter, who escapes from the American chain gang and becomes an emperor of the Island. He convinces the natives by telling that he can be killed only by a silver bullet which he possesses. Gradually the natives revolt and escapes to the jungle and encounters hallucinations and finally killed by the natives with a silver bullet prepared by them.

MAJOR CHARACTERS: Brutus Jones, the emperor of the Island; **Smithers,** is a cantankerous white sailor and a friend of Jones; **Lem,** is the chief of the natives on the island; **The Witch Doctor,** is an old man from Congo.

SETTING: *The Emperor Jones* is set in a Carribean Island, an unnamed island in the West Indies.

ADAPTATIONS: In 1933, the play was adapted into a feature film directed by Dudley Murphy, an avant-garde filmmaker of O'Neill's ***Greenwich Village circle*** who pursued the reluctant playwright for a decade before getting the rights from him.

SYMBOLS: Jones's Uniform represents Jones's emperorship, his disintegration symbolizes his return to humanity, **The Color White** is a symbol of power, **The Silver Bullet**, it represents Jones's tenuous hold on power, **The Crocodile God**, symbolically destroys his own godliness and his own good luck.

POINTS TO REMEMBER

- *The Emperor Jones* is a commentary on the United States' occupation of Haiti, and the play comments in broader terms on imperialism
- *The Emperor Jones* has become the standard American repertoire.

72. The Hairy Ape (1922)

AUTHOR: Eugene O'Neil

GENRE: Drama, Expressionism.

TITLE: The title *The Hairy Ape* refers to Yank, the central figure of the play, and his quest for identity or belongingness.

THEMES: Pride, Identity, and Belonging, Exploitation, Oppression, and the Individual, Aggression and Stupidity, Progress and Happiness.

PLOT: In *The Hairy Ape,* O'Neil explores class and identity as he presents the existential crisis of Yank, an engine worker for an ocean liner, who feels proud about his physical work. He was surprised and shocked with the remark of a rich industrialist that he resembles a wild beast makes him totally devastated. Yank realizes he has no place in modern society, so he tries to be friendly with a gorilla which in turn attacks and kills him.

MAJOR CHARACTERS: Yank, the protagonist of the play, a stoker who works on an ocean Liner; **Paddy**, an experienced old Irishman who works alongside Ocean Liner; **Mildred Dougla**s, the rich daughter of the president of Nazareth Steel; **Mildred's Aunt**, An old woman whom O'Neill describes as *" pompous and proud"*.

SETTING: The play begins on an ocean liner in NewYork City.

ADAPTATIONS: In 2017, Cannavale received a 2017 Obie Award for his performance for the stage production of play *The*

Hairy Ape in The Park Avenue Armory, directed by Richard Jones, and designed by Stewart Laing.

SYMBOLS: The stokehole, the foreman castle, the Fifth Avenue sky-scraper symbolise the contemporary materialistic cage in which man is imprisoned, **Mildred's White Dress** symbolizes her extreme privilege. **Yank** symbolises the animal nature in man, **The Hairy Ape** is a symbolic of deterioration Yank into an animal.

QUOTES

> "I'm thinking 'tis only slaves do be giving heed to the day that's gone or the day to come."

POINTS TO REMEMBER

- Dramatists like Elmer Rice and Eugene O'Neill introduced Expressionism to American Literature.
- *The Hairy Ape* is a portrayal of the impact industrialization and social class has on the dynamic character Yank.

73. Long Day's Journey into Night (1956)

AUTHOR: Eugene O'Neil

GENRE: Realistic Drama

TITLE: The title *The Long Day's Journey into Night* refers to the events of the play which happened in one day.

THEMES: Fatalism and Resignation, Denial, Blame, Guilt, Loneliness, Isolation, Belonging, Love and Forgiveness, the Past, Nostalgia, Regret.

PLOT: *The Long Day's Journey Into Night* is a semi-autobiographical family tragedy, portraying the mutually destructive relationships of drug addicted Mart Tyrone, her ex-actor husband James, and their two sons, hard- drinking Jamie and intellectual Edmund.

MAJOR CHARACTERS: James Tyrone, is the patriarch of the Tyrone family; **Mary Tyrone,** the matriarch of the Tyrone family; **Edmund Tyrone**, a 23 year old and youngest son of James and Mary; **Jamie Tyrone, a** failed actor addicted to drinking and the elder son of Tyrones; **Cathleen, the** housekeeper. Eugene Tyrone – James and Mary's second child.

SETTING: *The Long Day's Journey Into Night* is set in Tyrones' summer house, the seaside Connecticut in O' Neil's Monte Cristo Cottage, August 1912.

ADAPTATIONS: In 1996, film adaptation was directed by Canadian director David Wellington and starred William Hutt as

James, Martha Henry as Mary, Peter Donaldson as Jamie, Tom McCamus as Edmund and Martha Burns as Cathleen.

SYMBOLS: The Fog represents the ways in which isolation and separation manifest themselves within personal relationships. **Mary's Wedding Dress** is symbolic of the hope in Mary which will never again be able to relive.

 QUOTES: "We are such things as rubbish is made of, so let's drink up and forget it."

POINTS TO REMEMBER

- In 1957 O'Neill posthumously received Pulitzer Prize for his masterpiece *Long Day's Journey into Night.*
- *Long Day's Journey into Night* takes place on a single day in August 1912, from around 8:30 a.m. to midnight.
- *Long Day's Journey into Night* is an autobiographical play. All of the characters correspond to Eugene O'Neill's actual family members

74. *Who's Afraid of Virginia Woolf* (1962)

AUTHOR: Edward Elbee.

GENRE: Dramatic Stage play

TITLE: The title *Who is Afraid of Virginia Woolf* is a pun on the song *Who's Afraid of the Big Bad Wolf?* from Walt Disney's Three Little Pigs (1933), substituting the name of the celebrated English author Virginia Woolf. Martha and George repeatedly sing this version of the song throughout the play.

THEMES: Imperfect Marriage, Academia, Appearance, Secrecy, Truthtelling,Ambition, Success, and Failure, Reality versus Fantasy.

PLOT: *Who's Afraid of Virginia Woolf* is a play about the troubled marriage of a middle-aged couple named George, a professor of Maths in New England College & Martha invites the young couple Nick, who is a Zoology professor and his wife Honey. George and Martha indulge in personal violence and embarrases the guests and on liquor Martha Breaks their personal taboo about their son, an illusion accepted by the couple as self-defence against their impotency. Finally the couple comes out of the illusion and accepted the reality.

MAJOR CHARACTERS: Nick, is a new Biology professor; **Martha,** the daughter of the president of the college; **George,** an associate professor in the History; **Honey**, Nick's wife.

SETTING: The setting of the play is a township called New Carthage, a city where personal values are degraded and is also the setting of Edward Albee's plays.

ADAPTATIONS: The film adaptation was released in 1966, written by Ernest Lehman, directed by Mike Nichols, and starring Richard Burton, Elizabeth Taylor, George Segal and Sandy Dennis.

SYMBOLS: Babies Symbolise Martha and Honey's Infertility.

QUOTES

> "Musical beds is the faculty sport around here."
>
> "...who tolerates, which is intolerable; who is kind, which is cruel; who understands, which is beyond comprehension..."

POINTS TO REMEMBER

- Edward Elbee is the recipient of three Pulitzer Prizes for Drama, teaches playwriting at the University of Houston .
- In 1963,*Who is Afraid of Virginia Woolf* won the Tony award for the best play.
- The play is a critique on the American Family and their
- Albee has admitted that the resemblance of Nick's name to Nikita Kruschev—the Soviet premier—and of George's name to George Washington—first president and the icon of the American dream—were intentional.
- The play has three acts namely," **Fun and Games"**, **Walpurgisnacht"**(annualwitchesmeeting),**"The Exorcism"**

- In 2018, the Elevator Repair Service premiered a sequel written by Kate Scelsa, titled ***Everyone's Fine with Virginia Woolf***. This play introduces new plot elements such as vampirism.

75. *Raisin in the Sun (1959)*

AUTHOR: Lorraine Hansberry

GENRE: Drama, <u>Domestic tragedy</u>

TITLE: The title *Raisin in the Sun* comes from the poem *"Harlem"* (also known as "<u>A *Dream Deferred*")</u> by <u>*Langston Hughes*</u>." What happens to a dream deferred?/ Does it dry up/like raisin in the sun".

THEMES: Race relations, gender roles, God and generation gap, school vs work.

PLOT: *Raisin in the Sun* is a protest play or a social play portrays how a lower-class black family's struggle to gain middle-class acceptance by getting a house in white neighbourhood. When the play opens, Mama, the sixty-year-old mother of the family, is waiting for a $10,000 insurance check from the death of her husband, and the drama will focus primarily on how the $10,000 should be spent.

MAJOR CHARACTERS: Walter Lee Younger, the protagonist of the play, an aspiring businessman; **Lena Younger ("Mama")**, Walter and Beneatha's mother; **Beneatha Younger ("Bennie")**, the daughter and Walter's sister; **Ruth Younger**, Walter's wife and Travis's mother; **Joseph Asagai** - A Nigerian student in love with Beneatha.

SETTING: *Raisin in the Sun* is set in South Side, Chicago.

ADAPTATIONS: In 1961, a film version of *A Raisin in the Sun* was released. Hansberry wrote the screenplay, and was directed by

Daniel Petrie. Petrie received a special "Gary Cooper Award" at the Cannes Film Festival.

SYMBOLS: Music represents the culture and heritage, **Money** is a symbol for dreams and generational conflict, **Mama's plant and sunligh**t symbolise her nurturing of life in a small space, **Beneatha's hair** symbolises her pride as a black woman.

QUOTES

Man say to his woman: I got me a dream. His woman say: Eat your eggs.

Once upon a time freedom used to be life—now it's money.

POINTS TO REMEMBER:

- *Raisin in the Sun* is the first play written and directed by a black woman and director Mr. Richards to be produced on Broadway.

76. Fences (1985)

AUTHOR: August Wilson

GENRE: Drama

TITLE: The title *Fences* refers to the structure both literally and structurally that the characters build to keep others in and out of their lives

THEME: Fair play, Suppression, Responsibility

PLOT: The Play *Fences* focuses mainly on Troy, a 53-year-old man, who struggles for providing his family from the menial trash collecting. He is a Negro League Baseball player denied a chance to Major League Baseball because of the colour of his skin. So he doesn't want his son Cory to play football even though he is excellent in the game, causing a rift in the father son relationship. Cory enlists himself in Military and towards the end Cory pays his last respect to his father and understands his love for him.

MAJOR CHARACTERS: Troy Maxson , the protagonist of the play, **Rose Maxson,** loving and supportive wife, **Cory Maxson** , the son who tries to escape from his father's shadow, **Jim Bono,** Troy's friend, **Gabriel,** brother of Troy, who suffered injury from WW II,

SETTING: The play was set in 1957, at a backyard of a house in Pittsburgh, Pennsylvania.

ADAPTATIONS: In 2016 a film adaptation of Fences was directed by Denzel Washington.

SYMBOLS: Baseball, a complex symbol of fair play, injustice and freedom, **Fence**s, symbolizes Rose's goal

QUOTES: Some build fences to keep people out ... other(s) build fences to keep people in.

You can't visit the sins of the father upon the child.

POINTS TO REMEMBER:

- In 1987 *Fences* won the 1987 Pulitzer Prize for Drama and Tony Award for Best Play.

- The play was first developed at the Eugene O'Neill Theater Center's 1983 National Playwrights Conference and premiered at the Yale Repertory Theatre in 1985.

77. *The Lion and the Jewel (1959)*

AUTHOR: Wole Soyinka

GENRE: Drama

TITLE: The Title *The Lion and the Jewel* refers to the main characters Baroka as " Lion" and Sidi , the beauty as "Jewel".

THEME: Tradition Vs. Modernity, Men Vs. Women, Pride, Vanity, The Power Of Images, Language, Words.

PLOT: *The Lion and the Jewel* chronicles how Baroka, the village chief, who is the lion of the village, fights with the modern Lakunle over the right to marry Sidi, the titular Jewel. Lakunle is portrayed as the civilized antithesis of Baroka and unilaterally attempts to modernize his community and change its social conventions.

MAJOR CHARACTERS: Sidi, the village beauty of Ilujinle, **Lakunle,** the young school teacher in Ilujinle. Baroka, the Bale (village chief) of Ilujinle, **Sadiku,** the first and very loyal wife Baroka.

SETTING: Yoruba village of Ilujunle, a rural Nigerian village in the late 1950s

SYMBOLS: The magazine, symbolises women existence in Ilujinle, **The Statue Of Baroka,** symbolizes Baroka's power and vitality, **Postage Stamps** and **Camera** are symbolic of modernism

QUOTES:

"Romance is the sweetening of the soul

With fragrance offered by the stricken heart."

POINTS TO REMEMBER:

- In 1986, Wole Soyinka was awarded the Nobel Prize in Literature and he is the first black African to receive it.

- The play is divided into three parts namely, morning, noon and night.

- Wole Soyinka was the play reader in Royal Court Theatre, London where his plays are produced

- *The Interpreters* is the first novel by Wole Soyinka.

78. Death and the King's Horsemen (1975)

AUTHOR: Wole Soyinka

GENRE: Drama tragedy

TITLE: The title reads *"death"* as a separate character from *"the King's Horseman."* The most important role of death in the play is in fact not that of the King's Horseman, but rather the way death functions in both societies.

THEME: Life and Death, Woman and Power, Duty and Collective Responsibility, Colonialism

PLOT: *Death and the King's Horseman* is a play tells the story of Elesin, the king's horseman, who is expected to commit ritual suicide following the death of the king. He got distracted from his duty by the beauty of a young girl and was imprisoned and prevented from performing his duties by the colonial authorities. This brought failures to the horseman and he feels that the world will not see peace again.

MAJOR CHARACTERS: Elesin, is the titular horseman of the play, a vibrant man who due his role as the king's horseman, **Iyaloja**, the "mother of the market". **Olunde**, is Elesin's oldest son and the next King's Horesmen, **Simon and Jane Pilkings**, the colonist, **The praise-singer** is a man who accompanies Elesin, **Sergeant Amusa**, is a native Nigerian man a Islam Convert

SETTING: Oyo, Nigeria; sometime during World War II

SYMBOLS: European Music represents British colonialism.

QUOTES:

This market is my roost. When I come among the women I am a chicken with a hundred mothers.

POINTS TO REMEMBER:

- Death and the King's Horseman builds upon the true story of a horseman of Yoruba King.

- ***The Death and the King's Horseman*** embodies Wole Soyinka's post- Biafran cultural philosophy.

- The Swedish Academy drew special attention to *Death and the King's Horseman* and *Dance of the Forests*(1960) as evidence of Soyinka's talent for combining Yoruban and European culture into a unique kind of poetic drama.

- Soyinka examines the weaknesses of the Nigerian society, where people forget their traditions, culture, and their duty to themselves and to each other.

79. Dream on MonkeyMountain (1967)

AUTHOR: Derek Walcot(West Indian)

GENRE: Drama

TITLE: In the play *Dream on Monkey Mountain,* Derek Walcott describes the dream of the hero, which is a representation of Walcot himself.

THEME: Identity/Search for Self , Death and Rebirth ,Race and Racism

PLOT: In *Dream on Monkey Mountain* the central character, Makak, An old charcoal burner, who lives in Monkey Mountain was arrested for his drunken behaviour and imprisoned in a jail. Makak despises himself for being black and longs to lead his people back to Africa, where, in his dreams, he will become a fearless warrior and forgets his name attempts to rediscover himself by killing the white Goddess and the play ends with Malak returning to his monkey mountain with his friend.

MAJOR CHARACTERS: Basil is a black man (or perhaps apparition) who appears when death is imminent for someone, **Josephus** is the sick man who is healed by Makak, **Corporal Lestrade** runs the jail and is responsible for the arrest of Makak. **Makak** is the central character in the play, the one who has the dream on Monkey Mountain, **Moustique** is Makak's partner and friend in business and who accompanies him to Africa.

SETTING: West Indian jail, Carribean Island

SYMBOLS: Characters of African descent **Makak, Moustique, Souris, and Tigre** are the names of animals. They are monkey, mosquito, rat, and tiger, and it reveals their personality. **Basil** symbolise death, **White Woman** Symbolise Malak death in the end

QUOTES:

"Let them run ahead. Then I'll have good reason for shooting them down. Sharpeville? Attempting to escape. Attempting to escape from the prison of their lives. That's the most dangerous crime. It brings about revolution. So, off we go, lads!"

REVIEWS/CRITICISM: Edith Oliver, the journalist of *The New Yorker,* acclaimed the play as "a masterpiece" and "a poem in dramatic form or a drama in poetry".

POINTS TO REMEMBER:

- Walcott published his poetic masterpiece, ***Omerus***, a 325-page epic poem which gives a Caribbean twist to Homer's Iliad and Odyssey.
- In 1992, Walcott was awarded the Nobel Prize in Literature especially for poetry

80. *Mother Courage and Her Children (1941)*

AUTHOR: Bertolt Brecht, German Dramatist

GENRE: Satire, War Literature, Musical play

TITLE: Its title *Mother Courage and Her Children* refers to the ironic name given to the protagonist Anna Fierling, the courageous mother who runs the family with a very meager income from selling war supplies

THEME: Capitalism, Power Struggle, courage

PLOT: *Mother Courage and Her Children* is the antiwar musical stage-play written by exiled German dramatist Bertolt Brechtthe .The play is about Anna Fierling, who is addressed in the play as Mother courage, who runs a canteen business in a covered wagon selling alcohol to soldiers. She wants her children to be away from war and unfortunately, she lost all her children at the end of the play. The play concludes in 1636, with Mother Courage harnessing herself to the canteen-wagon. "I must get back into business," The play has 12 scenes which depicts the 12 years of her life.

MAJOR CHARACTERS: Mother Courage, the protagonist, the mother of Eliff, Kattrin and Swiss Cheese, **Kattrin,** courageous and tenderhearted daughter of Mother Courage, **Chaplin,** hypocritical Lutheran minister, who works for swedish army, **Eliff,** violent dishonest young man, **Swiss cheese,** honest military employee

SETTING: In Dalecarlia, a province in Sweden during thirty years war. It's 1624, six years since the start of the war.

ADAPTATIONS: In 1960 the play was adapted into a German movie in which his wife Helene Weigel, has cast.

SYMBOLS: Cart symbolise the perpetuation of war, **Yvette's Boot** symbolise love, **Drum** symbolise resistance to violence.

QUOTES:

> "I won't let you spoil my war for me. Destroys the weak, does it? Well, what does peace do for'em, huh? War feeds its people better."

> " Like the war to nourish you/ have to feed it something too"

POINTS TO REMEMBER:

- Bertolt Brecht Inaugurated the matured form of *epic theatre* and *Verfremdungseffekt*, ***Mother Courage and Her Children*** is an example to it.

- **Margarete Steffin,** the German actress and a prolific translator from Russian and Scandinavian languages has collaborated with Brecht in this play

- The central character Anna Fierling is drawn from a short novel, *The Runagate Courage,* by the German picaresque writer Grimmelshausen.

- *Mother Courage* was the inspiration for Lynn Nottage's Pulitzer winning play *Ruined.*

- The play has 12 scenes which depicts the 12 years of her life.

81. *The Life of Galileo (1940)*

AUTHOR: Bertolt Brecht

GENRE: Play, Agitprop (Political Propaganda), Epic Theater

TITLE: The title *The Life of Galileo* refers to the central character the famous astronomer Galileo.

THEME: Progress Vs. Tradition, Persecution, Ideas As Infection, Work Vs. Passion , Dogmatism Vs Science.

PLOT: *The Life of Galileo is a* play that portrays the excitement of the protagonist, Galileo, an eminent professor and scientist in the 17th century Venetian Republic about the world of science which turn out to be heretic to the orthodox world and he ends up as a prisoner of the Holy Inquisition and abjures his discoveries and theories.

MAJOR CHARACTERS: Galileo Galilei, the protagonist and title character, **Andrea Sarti**, a student of Galileo who gave the information about telescope, **The Little Monk,** member of the church who opposes the ideas of Galileo, **Federzoni**, grinds the lenses for Galileo Galilei's first telescope, **Cardinal Barberini**, who later became Pope Urban VIII.

SETTING: Venice, Florence, and Rome

ADAPTATIONS: The play *The Life of Galileo* has its first theatrical production in Germany and the production was directed by Leonard Steckel, the famous actor and stage director with set-design by Teo Otto. Steckel has casted himself as Galileo in the play.

SYMBOLS: APPLES symbolise forbidden knowledge, **THE PROVING STONE** represents the widely accepted knowledge that is wrong, **FIRE** symbolise rigorous questioning.

QUOTES:

You cannot teach a man anything; you can only help him find it within himself.

Wine is sunlight, held together by water.

Measure what is measurable, and make measurable what is not so.

I have never met a man so ignorant that I couldn't learn something from him.

The Bible shows the way to go to heaven, not the way the heavens go.

POINTS TO REMEMBER:

- Life of Galileo can be said to take place two times. The first is the time in which the play is set (Galileo's Italy in the 1600s), and the second is the time in which the play was written (Brecht's Europe in the 1930s).
- *The Life of Galileo* adheres closely to the real Galileo what is known about Galileo Galilei's intellectual convict with the Roman catholic church

82. *The Chairs (1952)*

AUTHOR: Eugène Ionesco

GENRE: One - Act play, Absurd play

TITLE: The title *The Chairs* takes its name from the chairs that the Old Man and Old Woman set up for their invisible guests

THEME: Absurdity, Human Condition/Isolation , Communication, nothingness

PLOT: In *The Chairs* elderly couple aged 95 and 94 lives in a house surrounded with water were playing a game of telling a story for 75 years. Tonight the old man has hired a professional orator to give a message in his story and have invited guests. When the orator comes the old couple is jumping out of excitement but the orator could not see them and he can only see empty chairs. The old couple jumped out of excitement through the window and drowned. The play ends with human voices of invisible crowd gradually subsided.

MAJOR CHARACTERS: The Old Man ,The Old Woman ,The Orator, who has been hired by the Old Man to deliver his message to the invisible crowd.

SETTING: The Chairs is a "tragic farce" (as Ionesco describes it), which takes place on a remote island. The play is not set in a particular time or place.

SYMBOLS: Semicircular stage, symbolizes the unseen and inaccessible past experience of the couple

QUOTES: "At the end, at the end of the end of the city of Paris, there was, there was, was what?"

POINTS TO REMEMBER:

- The play *The Chairs* is subtitled as the *Tragic farce*

83. *The Stranger (1942)*

AUTHOR: Albert Camus

GENRE: Absurd novel

TITLE: the title *The Stranger* refers to the protagonist of the play Merusault, who is a stranger to the customs and traditions of the society which makes him an outsider.

THEME: Meaningless and detached life, Miscommunication.

PLOT: *The Stranger* is about the protagonist Meursault, an indifferent young man who is an alienated self and strange to the values and traditions, attends his mother's funeral with her he always had a detached relationship. A few days later, he was sentenced to death as he kills Arab man in French Algiers. The plot is divided into two parts, presenting Meursault's narration and perspective before and after the murder.

MAJOR CHARACTERS: Merusault, alienated hero who thinks there is no meaning in life, **Marie Cardona**, young lover of Merusault, who values love and companionship, **Raymond Sintes**, abusive man, **Maman**, mother of Merusault, from whom he's detached, **Chaplain**, the priest.

SETTING: Algeria, a French Colony in North Africa

ADAPTATIONS: The novel was twice adapted as films: Lo Straniero (1967) (Italian) by Luchino Visconti and Yazgı (2001, Fate) by Zeki Demirkubuz (Turkish).

SYMBOLS: Courtroom represents society and traditional, **Crucifix**, symbolise the traditional christian belief about meaning of life, **Sun and Sea**, represents the hostile natural powers

QUOTES:

"I may not have been sure about what really did interest me, but I was absolutely sure about what didn't."

"I opened myself to the gentle indifference of the world."

"It is better to burn than to disappear."

"I had only a little time left and I didn't want to waste it on God."

POINTS TO REMEMBER:

- Camus view of nihilism is portrayed through the characterisation of Merusault, who thinks that nothing is relevant in this world.

- Camus explored what he termed "the nakedness of man faced with the absurd." in this novel and he was awarded the Nobel prize for literature in 1957

84. *The Plague (1947)*

AUTHOR: Albert Camus

GENRE: Allegory

TITLE: The title *The Plague* refers to the cruel plague that happened in Oran, Algeria

THEME: Human suffering, freedom, facing death

PLOT: *The Plague* tells the story of plague sweeping the French Algerian city of Oran. It asks a number of questions relating to the nature of destiny and the human condition. The characters in the book, ranging from doctors to vacationers to fugitives, all helps in presenting the cruelty and effects of plague on a populace.

MAJOR CHARACTERS: Dr. Bernard Rieux, the physician, **Jean Tarrou**, a journalist who visits Oran, **Joseph Grand**, a city employee who finds difficult to express, **Raymond Raubert**, journalist who tries to escape **Cottard**, a smuggler.

SETTING: *The Plague was set in* Port town of Oran Algeria.

SYMBOLS: Weather, represents indifference, **rats**, symbolize death, **plague**, represents suffering and alienation.

QUOTES:

"I know that man is capable of great deeds. But if he isn't capable of great emotion, well, he leaves me cold."

"They knew now that if there is one thing one can always yearn for, and sometimes attain, it is human love."

POINTS TO REMEMBER:

- The Plague is an allegory of the rise of fascism in Europe

- *The Plague* features the similarities between war and plague

- Albert Camus received nobel prize for literature in 1957

85. Hayavadana (1972)

AUTHOR: Girish Karnard

GENRE: Tragic comedy

TITLE: The title of the play, *Hayavadana* means, haya means horse/body and *vadana* means man/ head.

THEME: Identity, Hybridity, Incompleteness, Mind vs Body, Metatheatre and Storytelling, Indian Culture and Nationalism

PLOT: The play *Hayavadana* is a story of kapila, the ironsmith and Devadatta, the poet. Both Kapila and Devadatta happened to love Padmini. Both the friends cut their heads for her love and through the intervention of **Kali** the heads and bodies are transposed. Padmini lives with devadatta's head and Kapila's body.

MAJOR CHARACTERS: **The Bhagavata,** serves as the narrator. **Devadatta,** the poet, **Kapila, the** son of ironsmith, **Padmini,** the girl loved by both friends, **Hayavadana** – human body with a horse face. Hayavadana's name is apt, as it literally means " Horse Face".

SETTING: City of Dharmapura, mythical past

SYMBOLS: **The fortunate lady's flower**, symbolises limitations of Padmini's happiness in her marriage, **MASKS,** represents the incompleteness of Character

QUOTES:

"O single-tusked destroyer of incompleteness, we pay homage to you and start our play."

"Two friends there were—one mind, one heart. They saw a girl and forgot themselves. But they could not understand the song she sang."

POINTS TO REMEMBER:

- Received the Jnanpith Award, India's highest literary honor, in 1999
- Girish karnad drew inspiration for Hayavadana from Thomas Mann 1940 novella *The Transposed Heads.*

86. *Silence! The Court is in Session* (1967)

AUTHOR: Vijay Tendulkar

GENRE: Modern Drama

TITLE: The title *Silence the Court Is in Session* is symbolic. The word **"silence"** symbolizes the patriarchal society which silences the voice of woman in the name of social justice and ideology. **The court** symbolizes a repressive law system sanctioned by the state.

THEME: Performance And Self Expression ,Women's Roles In Society, Middle Class Status, Tradition, And Propriety , Guilt And Innocence

PLOT: The play *Silence the court is in session is* about a group of teachers planning to stage a play in a village. They did a mock trial as one of the cast-members does not show up. A local stagehand is asked to replace him to understand court procedures. A (mock) charge of infanticide is leveled against Miss Benare, Gradually, the mock trial turns into an accusatory game when it emerges from the trial that Miss Benare is carrying an out-of-wedlock child from her failed illicit relationship with Professor Damle, the missing cast-member.

MAJOR CHARACTERS: Benare, the play's protagonist Leela Benare is an unmarried teacher, **Samant**, is a local villager, **Sukhatme**, central member of the Living Courtroom, who plays lawyer for the prosecution, **Ponkshe**, a failed academic who works as a clerk, **Mr. Kashikar,** who plays as judge, **Professor Damle**, professor who has an affair with Benare.

SETTING: A community center in a village in India

ADAPTATIONS: In 1971 Satyadev Dubey, the Marathi playwright adapted into a Marathi film named ***Shantata! Court Chalu Aahe***, which started the New Cinema movement in Marathi cinema ·

SYMBOLS: The Locked Door, symbolise the inescapability from persecution,

Sparrow represents Benare, **The sparrow's nest,** symbolises the safe house, **Silence** ! symbolises the forceful quieting of woman

QUOTES:

"What I say is, our society should revive the old custom of child marriage. Marry off the girls before puberty. All this promiscuity will come to a full stop."

 POINTS TO REMEMBER:

- Silence! The Court is in Session is based on the 1956 Swiss novel Die Panne, known as A Dangerous Game in English.

87. *To Kill a Mockingbird (1960)*

AUTHOR: Harper Lee

GENRE: Southern Gothic and Bildungsroman novel, Domestic Fiction, Legal Story

TITLE: *To Kill a Mockingbird*, the title is a metaphor that relates to the idea of the destruction of innocence of Boo Radley and Tom Robinson, who are innocent of the accusations on them. These two characters are the true Mockingbirds of the story.

THEME: Racial injustice and the destruction of innocence, class

PLOT: The story of *To Kill a Mockingbird* was narrated by Jean Louise, the daughter of lawyer Atticus. Jean along with her brother Jem and her friend Dill are excited by their neighbour Boo Radley. In the meantime Atticus was given the job to defend a negro Tom Richardson, who is charged with the crime of raping a white girl. Consequently he evoked anger from his own community for helping the negro as a result his children were attacked and Boo rescued the children and their fascination for the neighbour increases.

MAJOR CHARACTERS: Jean Louise ("Scout") Finch, a six year old girl, who in intelligent though unconventional, **Jeremy Atticus** ("Jem"), her brother, **Atticus Finch**, the father and lawyer,

Tom Robinson, negro accused of raping a white woman named **Mayella Ewell**, the white woman, **Bob Ewell**, Mayella's father.

SETTING: *To Kill a Mockingbird is set* in the fictional withered old town of Maycomb, Alabama, the seat of Maycomb County.

ADAPTATIONS: In 1962, Robert Mulligan adapted into an Academy Award-winning film   with a screenplay penned by Horton Foote.

SYMBOLS: mockingbird symbolise   innocence, **Boo Radley,** symbolises virtue of people.

QUOTES:

"You never really understand a person until you consider things from his point of view... Until you climb inside of his skin and walk around in it."

"Until I feared I would lose it, I never loved to read. One does not love breathing."

"I think there's just one kind of folks. Folks."

REVIEWS/CRITICISM: In 2006, British librarians ranked the book ahead of the <u>Bible</u> as one "every adult should read before they die".

POINTS TO REMEMBER:

- It has won the Pulitzer Prize and become a classic of modern American literature.

- Lee stated that To Kill a Mockingbird is an example of how an author "should write about what he knows and write truthfully".

- Lee modeled the character of Dill on Capote, based on her childhood friend known as Truman Persons

- In 1964 interview, Lee revealed that her aspiration was "to be ... the Jane Austen of South Alabama."

- In November 5,2007, the then President George W. Bush awarded Lee with the Presidential Medal of Freedom for ***To Kill a Mockingbird***

88. Dance Like a Man (2000)

AUTHOR: Mahesh Dattani

GENRE: Drama

TITLE: *Dance Like a Man* the title suggests the association of dance with women and femininity and also suggests the susceptibility in man's identity.

THEME: Gender discrimination, Sufferings, suppression, Stereotypical attitude, ambition and social construct.

PLOT: *Dance Like a Man* explores the life of a budding dancer, Jairaj, and how he loses his career. The plot revolves around three generations. Jairaj and Ratna want to develop their career as Bharatanatyam dancers and their personal ambition, sacrifices, struggle and compromises, internal conflict and the way they cope up with life and dance being the major topic of discussion in the house as it is a topic of debate between the father and his son and daughter in-law.

MAJOR CHARACTERS: Jairaj, he is a Bharatanatyam dancer **,Ratna** the wife of Jairaj, who belongs to the Devadasi community, **Amritlal , the** father of Jairaj, **Lata** , Jayaraj and Ratna's daughter, who is also a dancer.

SETTING: *Dance like a Man* the play is set in an ancestral house in Parekh

SYMBOLS: The shawl stands as a symbol pride for Amirtlal but to Jairaj it symbolise his unfulfilled desire to be recognised as a dancer.

QUOTES: "A woman is man's world is considered progressive, but a man is a woman's world is considered pathetic."

POINTS TO REMEMBER:

- **Mahesh Dattani** is the first playwright to receive *Sahitya Academy Award*
- *In Dance Like a Man,* Dattani makes use of the flashback technique and the split-scene device.

89. Interpreter of Maladies (1999)

AUTHOR: Jhumpa Lahari

GENRE: Short stories, fiction

TITLE: *Interpreter of Maladies* takes its title from one of the stories in the collection. In that story, Mr. Kapasi's full-time job as a doctor's assistant involves translating from one Indian language to another so that the patients can communicate their symptoms and complaints. It is symbolic of the characters physical or psychological disorders or maladjustments.

THEME: The Difficulty of Communication, The Danger of Romanticism, multiculturalism, alienation,

MAJOR CHARACTERS: Mr. and Mrs. Das, Indian Americans visiting the country of their heritage, **Mr. Kapasi** as their driver for the day as they tour.

SETTING: India, America, New England

SYMBOLS: The Camera, Mr. Das's camera represents his inability to see the world clearly, **Mrs. Das's Puffed Rice**, represents her shortcomings and careless actions.

QUOTES:

> "Sexy means loving someone you do not know."

> "A woman who had fallen out of love with her life"

> "As strange as it seemed, I knew in my heart that one day her death would affect me, and stranger still, that mine would affect her."

REVIEWS/CRITICISM: In June 1999 the San Francisco chronicle opined on her method as "story telling of surpassing kindness and skill"

POINTS TO REMEMBER:

- In 2000, *Interpreter of Maladies* won the Pulitzer Prize for Fiction and the Hemingway Foundation/PEN Award.

- The stories are about the lives of Indians and Indian Americans who are caught between their roots and the "New World."

- She also argues that Interpreter of Maladies is not just a collection of random short stories that have common components, but a "short story cycle" in which the themes and motifs are intentionally connected to produce a cumulative effect on the reader:

90. Dubliners (1914)

AUTHOR: James Joyce

GENRE: Short stories

TITLE: *Dubliners* takes its title from the characters in the stories that make up the collection. Each story focuses on a resident of Dublin, Ireland.

THEME: Religion, escape, Identity,class.

PLOT: *Dubliners i*s a naturalistic depiction of the Irish middle class in the twentieth century. It is a typical portrait of the nation.

MAJOR CHARACTERS: Child narrator ("Araby"), Eveline,Little Chandler, Mrs. Mooney, the titular owner in In "The Boarding House, "Maria, Tom Kernan, Gabriel Conroy

SETTING: City of Dublin, Ireland.

SYMBOLS: Food, is a typical symbol in literature that reinforces bonds between people, **Alcohol**, represent an occasion for forming social bonds, **Weather**, reflect the mindset of characters

QUOTES:

"Too excited to be genuinely happy"

"There's no friends like the old friends."

POINTS TO REMEMBER:

- It is far more accessible and often serves as a gateway into Joyce's world.

- A naturalistic depiction of Irish middle class life in and around Dublin in the early years of the 20th century.

- All characters of **Dubliners** centre on Joyce's idea of an epiphany: a moment where a character experiences a life-changing self-understanding or illumination.

- The child protagonist is the narrator in the first part.

91. I Know Why the Caged Birds Sing

AUTHOR: Marguerite Johnson known as Maya Angelou

GENRE: Autobiography, coming-of-age story

TITLE: The book's title ***"I Know Why the Caged Bird Sings*** is taken from a poem by African-American poet Paul Laurence Dunbar. The caged bird, a symbol for the chained slave, is an image Angelou uses throughout all her writings.

THEME: Discrimination, child molestation, self-esteem, family

PLOT: ***"I Know Why the Caged Bird Sings"*** is a heartfelt biography of Maya Angelou. It is about her childhood and teenage years. It is her story of discrimination, poverty, strength, and hope. The book opens with three-year-old Maya and her older brother are sent to Stamps, Arkansas, to live with their grandmother and concludes with Maya becoming a mother at the age of 16.

MAJOR CHARACTERS: Marguerite Johnson, the author Maya Angelou, the primary character in the book, **Bailey Johnson Jr.** is Maya's brother, Annie **Henderson,** father of Maya and Bailey, Vivian Baxter is the mother of Maya and Bailey. **Grandma Baxter**, the mother of Vivian and the grandmother of Maya and Bailey. **Mr. Freeman**, is Victoria Baxter's boyfriend who molests Maya, **Bertha Flowers** is a wealthy black woman who likes Maya in Stamps.

SETTING: The novel is set in different places during different actions. At early age at Stamps, Arkansas, the days with their mother at St. Louis, Missouri,San Francisco, California when maya is in preteen, Southern California , her life in junkyard.

SYMBOLS: Bird struggling to escape its cage, described in Paul Laurence Dunbar's poem, as a prominent symbol throughout her series of autobiographies **The Store**, becomes a symbol for her grandmother's power, **Stamps and Arkansas**, is a symbol of discrimination and despair, **Books**, symbolise Maya's way of escaping from life, **Boxing** symbolise the struggle of blacks during times of discrimination. **The San Francisco Streetcar Company** becomes a symbol for Maya's own abilities and dreams. **Railroad Trucks,** a symbol of escape for Bailey and Maya, **Easter Dress** is a symbol of her which she believes to make her beautiful.

QUOTES: I make writing as much a part of my life as I do eating or listening to music.

POINTS TO REMEMBER:

- Angelou has described William Shakespeare as a strong influence on her life and works, and claiming that "Shakespeare was a black woman".

- James Baldwin (1955), Angelou's friend and mentor, called Caged Bird "a Biblical study of life in the midst of death".

- Angelou reciting her poem "On the Pulse of Morning" at US President Bill Clinton's inauguration, January 20, 1993making her first poet to make an inaugural recitation since Robert Frost at the inauguration of John F. Kennedy in 1961.

- US President Barack Obama presenting Angelou with the Presidential Medal of Freedom, 2011 the highest civilian award

92. The Myth of Sisyphus (1942)

AUTHOR: Albert Camus

GENRE: Philosophical essay

TITLE: Camus uses the Greek legend of Sisyphus, who is condemned by the gods for eternity to repeatedly roll a boulder up a hill only to have it roll down again once he got it to the top, as a metaphor for the individual's persistent struggle against the essential absurdity of life.

THEME: Absurdism and Meaning, Humankind and The Natural World, Masculinity, Philosophy and Art

PLOT: In The Myth of Sisyphus, Albert Camus aims to draw out his definition of absurdism and strategies which are available to people in living with the absurd.

MAJOR CHARACTERS: Sisyphus, Albert Camus, Don Juan, is Albert Camus' first example of an 'absurd man', **The Actor,** the actor-figure as another 'absurd man', **The Conqueror,** is Albert Camus' third 'absurd man', **Kirilov,** is a character that Camus discusses in the 'absurd creation', **Fyodor Dostoevsky,** is a 19th Century Russian novelist, **Soren Kierkegaard,** is a 19th century Danish philosopher.

SYMBOLS: Sisyphus' rock represents mankind's absurd dilemma.

QUOTES:

> "In order to understand the world, one has to turn away from it on occasion."

"Seeking what is true is not seeking what is desirable."

"Man is always prey to his truths. Once he has admitted them, he cannot free himself from them."

POINTS TO REMEMBER:

- In 1957 Albert Camus was awarded the Nobel Prize for Literature and he is the second youngest recipient after Rudyard Kipling.

- Albert Camus adapted William Faulkner's *Requiem for a Nun* to stage in 1956

- The English translations of his french version of **The Myth Of Sisyphus** was done by Justin O'Brien in 1955.

- Camus further argues that with the joyful acceptance of the struggle against defeat, the individual gains definition and identity.

- *The Theatre of Absurd* is a word coined by Martin Esslin.

93. *The Bear Came Over the Mountain (1999)*

AUTHOR: Alice Munro

GENRE: Short story, Realism, Southern Ontario Gothic

THEME: Love, Fidelity and Marriage, Memory, Aging, Identity, Gender and Power, Class, Practicality.

PLOT: "*The Bear Came Over the Mountain*", is a story of love between Grant and Fiona, who in latter part her life is affected with Alziemer disease. It is a story that interweaves the tale of two couples who meet by chance and its consequences because of their involvement in each other's lives.

MAJOR CHARACTERS: Grant, a retired professor of Anglo-Saxon and Nordic literature, **Fiona**, Grant's wife, **Aubrey**, a temporarily resident at Meadow lake, **Marian**, is Aubrey's wife, **Kristy**, the main nurse .

SETTING: Huron country Ontario, Canada

ADAPTATIONS: In 2006 *The Bear Came Over the Mountain* was adapted into a critically acclaimed and oscar nominated film **Away From Her**, by Canadian writer and director Sarah Polley.

SYMBOLS: **Fiona's hair** is a symbol of her identity and individuality, **Drapes**, symbolize the class difference

POINTS TO REMEMBER:

- In 2013, The Swedish Academy awarded Alice Munro, the Canadian short story writer with the Nobel prize for literature and called her "master of the contemporary short story"
- She also won the Man Booker International prize in 2009.
- Alice Munro style of delving into the intricate nature of man in a simple style reminds the readers of Anton Chekov.

94. *The Snows of Kilimanjaro (1936)*

AUTHOR: Ernest Hemingway

GENRE: Tragedy

TITLE: The title refers to Mt. Kilimanjaro, a snow-capped mountain and dormant volcano in Tanzania (a country in East Africa). At 19,341 feet, Mt. Kilimanjaro is Africa's tallest peak. In many of his works Hemingway uses mountains to represent purity and goodness

THEME: Death and Decay, Postwar Trauma and Loss

PLOT: *The Snows of Kilimanjaro* starts with an epigraph, a short, pithy observation about a lone leopard who sought the tip of Kilimanjaro (literally, "The House of God"). Harry and his wife are stranded in a safari in Africa and are waiting for a rescue plane which Harry is sure it won't. He recollects his past life and he regrets that he has wasted his talents and skills for the material prosperity offered by his rich wife.

MAJOR CHARACTERS: Compton, a pilot who exists only in Harry's dream, **Harry,** the protagonist and a writer and has bitter experiences of war, **Helen,** the wealthy woman and the wife of Harry, **Molo,** the African servant.

SETTING: *The Snows of Kilimanjaro* is set in African Savannah

ADAPTATIONS: In 1952 *The Snows of Kilimanjaro* was adapted into a film directed by Henry King with a different climax.

SYMBOLS: Snow, Harry associates snow with Christmas celebrations, **lights, Mountaintop**, symbolises the search for deeper meaning in life, **Leopard**, symbolise immortality, **Hyena**, symbolises savagery and death, **Vultures**, symbolise Harry's death.

QUOTES:

"I'll have all I want. Not all I want but all there is."

"However, you make your living is where your talent lies."

POINTS TO REMEMBER:

- In ***The Snows of Kilimanjaro,*** the character Harry is loosely based on writer F. Scott Fitzgerald, who wrote about the upper classes in work *The Great Gatsby*.

- An opening epigraph describes Mt. Kilimanjaro's stature and significance in Africa as the "House of God."

- Hemingway was awarded the nobel prixze in the year 1954

95. *The Beast in the Jungle (1903)*

AUTHOR: Henry James

GENRE: Novella   Allegory, Romance, Tragedy

TITLE: The title **The Beast in the Jungle** refers to the neurotic obsession of John Marcher   that something worse is going to happen in his life like a beast hiding in a jungle, waiting for its prey.

THEME: Isolation, love, fear,

PLOT: *The Beast in the Jungle* is a story of John Marcher who awaits his fate which was partially informed to him by his friend May, who dies and reveals to him that this is his fate that he loses her.

MAJOR CHARACTERS: John Marcher is a member of the upper class in Britain, **May Bartram** is a caring, warm woman who first acts as host and a caretaker.

SETTING: Stately English home Weatherend

ADAPTATIONS: In 2018 the novella was adapted into a film by Dutch director <u>Clara van Gool</u>.

SYMBOLS: The Beast represents John Marcher's fate, **Calendar**, symbolise various meanings, **Sphinx**, represents Marcher's idea or wish of May becoming omniscient.

QUOTES:

"I'll watch with you."

"What if she should have to die before knowing, before seeing ...?"

POINTS TO REMEMBER:

- In "The Beast in the Jungle," readers can see John Marcher's fatalistic attitude toward life.

- *The Beast in the Jungle is a* confession on his own life.

- Sylvia plath, the American poet, has made a reference to *The Beast in the Jungle is* her sonnet , "<u>Ennui</u>" (2006)

Works Consulted

Books

Albert, Edward, History of English Literature. 5th edition. 1923. Oxford. Oxford UP, 1979.

Daiches, David. A Critical History of English Literature. 2 vols. New Delhi: Allied,1979.

Nayar, Pramod K. A Short History of English Literature. Bangalore: Foundation Books, 2009.

Sanders, Andrew. The Short Oxford History of English Literature. London: Oxford UP,2000.

Vallath, Kalyani. AContemporary Encyclopedia of British Literature. 3vols.Trivandrum: Bodhi Tree Books,2021.

Websites

The Norton Anthology of English Literature

Encyclopedia Britannica

Project Gutenberg

Spark Notes

Cliff Notes

English Literature on the Web

SIRENS AND SEA CAPTAINS

From the Realms of Lurin Series

A Romantic Regency-inspired Fantasy

Written by
COURTNEY DENELSBECK